THE PERSIANS

LOST CIVILIZATIONS

The books in this series explore the rise and fall of the great civilizations and peoples of the ancient world. Each book considers not only their history but their art, culture and lasting legacy and asks why they remain important and relevant in our world today.

Already published:

The Indus Andrew Robinson
The Persians Geoffrey Parker and Brenda Parker

THE
PERSIANS
LOST CIVILIZATIONS

GEOFFREY PARKER
AND BRENDA PARKER

REAKTION BOOKS

This book is dedicated to our six grandchildren:
Ben, Max, Zoe, Geoffrey, Maddy and Spike.

Published by Reaktion Books Ltd
Unit 32, Waterside
44–48 Wharf Road
London N1 7UX, UK

www.reaktionbooks.co.uk

First published 2017

Printed and bound in China by 1010 Printing International Ltd

A catalogue record for this book is available from the British Library

ISBN 978 1 78023 650 6

CONTENTS

CHRONOLOGY

587 BC	Jerusalem falls to the Babylonian king Nebuchadnezzar II The Babylonian Captivity of the Jews begins
550 BC	Death of Cambyses I of Anshan and succession of Cyrus II
528 BC	Buddhism founded by Siddhartha Gautama
521 BC	Darius I succeeds Cyrus
457–429 BC	Golden Age of Athens under Pericles
431 BC	Beginning of the Peloponnesian Wars between Athens and Sparta
332 BC	Alexander the Great founds Alexandria
331 BC	Alexander the Great defeats Darius III and conquers Persian Empire

270 BC	Conquest of Italy by Rome
221 BC	Chin Shih Huang-ti establishes the Chinese Empire
146 BC	Rome defeats and destroys Carthage
AD 27	Founding of the Roman Empire
c. AD 29	Crucifixion of Jesus of Nazareth
116	The Roman Emperor Trajan conquers Mesopotamia
226	Sasanid dynasty in Persia
313	The Roman emperor Constantine accepts Christianity
320	The Gupta dynasty unifies northern India
330	Constantinople, built on the site of Byzantium, becomes the capital of the Roman Empire
360	Hun invasion of Europe
395	Division of the Roman Empire between East and West
476	Barbarian conquest of the western Roman Empire
610	Beginning of the religion of Islam

642	The Arabs defeat the Persian army at the battle of Nehawand
771	Charlemagne (Charles the Great) becomes king of the Franks and establishes the state which will become known as the Holy Roman Empire
850	The Norseman Rurik becomes the ruler of Kiev
1096	The First Crusade and the establishment of the Christian kingdom of Jerusalem
1206	Establishment of the sultanate of Delhi. Mongol chieftain Temujin is proclaimed Genghis Khan and begins his conquests. Establishment of the Mongol Yuan dynasty in China. The Mongols rule the country until 1368
1290	Founding of the Ottoman Empire
1368	Defeat of the Mongols in China and establishment of the Ming dynasty
1380	Tamerlane conquers Persia
1421	Beginning of the Portuguese explorations under Henry the Navigator
1453	Constantinople falls to the Ottomans and becomes their capital
1526	Founding of the Mughal dynasty in India

1707	Death of the emperor Aurangzeb and beginning of the disintegration of the Mughal Empire
1739	The Persian Nadir Shah invades India, sacks Delhi and takes the Peacock Throne back to Persia where it becomes the new symbol of the shahs
1757	Victory in the Battle of Plassey results in Britain becoming the major power in north India
1858	India's First War of Independence (the Indian Mutiny) results in the British Crown taking over the responsibilities of the East India Company
1869	Opening of the Suez Canal produces renewed British interest in the Middle East
1876	Queen Victoria becomes Empress of India. Britain is now the dominant power in southern Asia
1900	Boxer Rebellion in China and almost complete take over of the country by the great powers – Britain, Russia and Germany
1908	Founding of the Anglo-Persian Oil Company
1914–18	The First World War results in the fall of the German, Austrian, Russian and Ottoman empires which have dominated Europe and the Middle East during the nineteenth century. Britain and France become the dominant powers in the Middle East

1922	Establishment of the Soviet Union
1925	Reza Shah founds the Pahlavi dynasty in Persia
1931	Japanese invasion of Manchuria, which eventually leads to the Japanese conquest of much of China
1939–45	Second World War produces the two 'super-powers' – the United States and the Soviet Union. They dominate the world scene throughout most of the rest of the twentieth century
1943	Tehran is the first meeting place of the 'Big Three' – Britain, the United States and the Soviet Union
1950s–60s	Those Middle Eastern states that had been reduced to quasi-colonial status by Britain and France gain their independence
1972	Great ceremonies in Iran in an attempt to resurrect the ancient empire
1980	Establishment of the Islamic Republic of Iran followed by war with Iraq
1991	Fall of the Soviet Union
2001	Destruction of the World Trade Center in New York triggers the outbreak of conflict in the Middle East. Invasion of Afghanistan and later Iraq by American-led alliance of Western powers

A frieze showing archers, from the palace of Darius I at Susa, excavated by Marcel Dieufalo, 1885–6.

LOST AND FOUND

The land of Persia, which officially changed its name to Iran in the 1930s, is the location of an ancient civilization dating back to the first millennium BC. However, despite the fact that Persia is closer to Europe than most of the rest of Asia, and in ancient times had close, although usually hostile, relations with the ancient Greeks and Romans, it is not at all well known. Over the centuries pickings have been taken from Persian poets, such as Edward Fitzgerald's translation of the *Rubaiyat of Omar Khayyam*, but such things have usually been seen as little more than curiosities from the mysterious East.

This is largely because in the context of European history, Persia has been considered 'the other', the Asiatic, which was very different from that Graeco-Roman civilization that was basic to the development and culture of Europe. In this context, 'the other' has been something largely unknown, often disturbing and usually dangerous. Throughout history, it has very often been in conflict with the Europeans. Persia was the first country to assume this role around the middle of the first millennium BC, and it was the Persians' enemies the Greeks who gave early Europe its first indication of how different the people of Persia were.

With the arrival of Islam in the seventh century, the idea of the East as 'the other' was reinvigorated and gained a new religious dimension. The whole of the Islamic world was in this category and this, of course, included Persia.

Many centuries later, the pioneering of sea routes to the East by the early navigators from western Europe led to the discovery that there was a route to India round the south of Africa. As a result, by the sixteenth century the Middle East, which until then had been very much 'the East' in the European mind, became a backwater, and attention moved further east. It was not until the opening of the Suez Canal in 1868 that the situation once more changed and the new Mediterranean–Red Sea route eastwards resulted in a renewed interest, and concern with, this region. However, for the Europeans, by then mainly involved in trade with South and East Asia, the Middle East was still only the location of a new and shorter routeway and was of little real interest in itself. During the late nineteenth century, the Middle East, including Persia, had only the most minor of roles in that new imperial world which had been created by the Europeans.

In the early twentieth century this all changed as a result of an important technological development, the invention of the internal combustion engine, which by the middle of the century was to replace most existing methods of transport. Oil was the fuel for this new engine and while supplies were at first obtained from a number of different places, most notably southern Russia, these proved to be inadequate for a number of reasons. Much exploration took place and it was not long before oil was discovered in large quantities in the Middle East.

The first of this oil was found by British prospectors in Persia and in no time the Anglo-Persian, later Anglo-Iranian, Oil Company was established. This company proceeded to build a massive oil refinery at Abadan on the southern coast of the country, which was soon shipping refined oil to Britain.

As a result there was a new surge of interest in Persia. This time it was related to the physical resource, which had become of the greatest importance to Britain and to the maintenance of her place as a great imperial power in the world. It was deemed essential that Iranian oil should continue to be exploited for the benefit of Britain, which meant that it was necessary for the country to be brought firmly into the British sphere. Associated with this was a renewed interest in the Persian language and this inevitably led to a knowledge – if not real understanding – of Persian history, legends and literature. While the country was never part of the British Empire, it rapidly moved into the British sphere of influence. The greatest empire in the ancient world had now become a small part of the sphere of the greatest empire of modern times.

This period of subservience lasted throughout most of the twentieth century and only ended as a result of the revival of the ideology of Islam. By that time the United States had taken over from Britain as the dominant power in the Middle East, although Iran continued to be the major supplier of oil to Britain. In 1980 the Islamic Republic of Iran came into being and subservience to the West abruptly ended. This Islamic Republic was from the outset hostile to the West and immediately demonstrated its own ambitions to become once more a world power of some significance. By the twenty-first century this even included the possibility of becoming a nuclear power. This all presented Western powers with a new and for them threatening situation in which another power had been added to those they considered a danger to the still Western-dominated world order.

While this new Iran was still part of the wider Islamic world, which was increasingly being split by its own challenges, it held a unique position. It had its own distinct cultural attributes, setting it apart from the dominant Arab culture of most of the rest of the Middle East, and it had also developed its own particular version of Islam. This Shia version of Islam was never accepted by the dominant Sunni Arabs, but was one of the factors that made Iran different from its neighbours. However, most of the country's characteristic features can be traced back to pre-Islamic times, in some cases even as far back as the country's early civilization. Many of these have been rediscovered by the Islamic Republic and have been incorporated into its distinctive structure.

This book will examine the country's ancient civilization and consider the ways in which the memory of it has persisted through the ages. Although in one sense 'lost', it has throughout its history been many times 'found' and has left its mark on the country as it is today.

Portrait of King Jamshid, signed by Mihr' Ali, Persia, Qajar dynasty, dated AD 1803.

ONE

Origins: The Land and the People

T he land into which the ancient Persians moved during the second millennium BC was the belt of alpine mountains which swathe the western and southern fringes of the great plains of Central Asia. These stretch from Europe to East Asia and in most places they consist of two or more enormous ranges separated by high plateaux. In the land occupied by the Persians these ranges are generally aligned in a west-to-east direction. In the north the main mountain range is the Kuhha-ye Alborz – the Alborz – which is part of a sequence of ranges stretching from Anatolia to Afghanistan. The highest mountains of this range lie to the south of the Caspian Sea and the highest peak is Mount Damavand, which reaches a height of 5,601 metres. Damavand is also the highest mountain in the Middle East and the Alborz range constitutes a formidable barrier to movement in the north of the Persian lands.

Lying to the south of this range and separated from it by a series of plateaux is the Kuhha-ye Zagros, the Zagros range. This is a complex series of mountains with a number of peaks reaching over 4,500 metres. The plateaux separating these two alpine ranges are for the most part between 1,000 and 1,500 metres in height. The plateaux are themselves crossed by a number of smaller ranges. The most important of these are the Kuhha-ye Qohrud, which separate the eastern deserts from the rest of the country. On the southwestern flank of the northern Zagros range lies the great fluvial basin of Mesopotamia, drained by the Tigris and Euphrates rivers. Here the land is far lower than the rest of Iran and consequently the overall conditions are very different.

The climate of the country is continental, with considerable annual extremes of temperature and in most places relatively low rainfall. Isfahan, the former capital in the heart of the country lying just to the north of the Zagros range at a height of 1,773 metres, has average temperatures of below zero throughout the winter months, rising to over 30 degrees Celsius during the summer. The annual rainfall is 108 mm and between June and September there is no recorded rainfall. The present capital, Tehran, situated on the southern flanks of the Alborz mountains at a height of 1,220 metres, has similar sub-zero temperatures in the winter with again temperatures rising to over 30 degrees in the summer. The temperature ranges of these two places are very similar but Tehran's rainfall of 250 mm is far higher than that of Isfahan and there is no month without recorded rainfall.

In general, the continental features of the climate, with extremes of temperature and low average rainfall, are most in evidence on the central plateaux, while the north adjacent to the

CLIMATE STATISTICS OF IRAN

Climate of Isfahan (1,773 m)				
Month	Temperature °c			Average Monthly Precipitation (mm)
	Average Daily		Highest Recorded	Lowest Recorded
	Max	Min		
January	8	-4	18	-19	15
July	37	19	42	9	0

Climate of Tehran (1,220 m)				
Month	Temperature °c			Average Monthly Precipitation (mm)
	Average Daily		Highest Recorded	Lowest Recorded
	Max	Min		
January	7	-3	18	-21	46
July	37	22	43	15	3

Climate of Abadan (2 m)				
Month	Temperature °c			Average Monthly Precipitation (mm)
	Average Daily		Highest Recorded	Lowest Recorded
	Max	Min		
January	17	7	25	-3	38
July	44	28	50	23	0

Physical map of Iran and the adjacent parts of the Middle East.

Caspian Sea and the south constituting the northern shore of the Persian Gulf have heavier rainfall and generally far less extreme temperatures. The centre of the plateau consists of the Dasht-e Kavir (Great Salt Desert) in the north and the Dasht-e Lut (Great Sand Desert) in the east. Surrounded as they are by the northern and southern mountain ranges, these are some of the driest lands in the world, subject to long periods of complete drought and fierce sandstorms. Mesopotamia to the west of the Zagros has many climatic differences and far fewer extremes of temperature.

The natural vegetation cover of Iran is very varied. While the lower lands around the mountains support forms of steppe grassland, the high mountains themselves support only plants characteristic of alpine environments. Since the centre of the plateau consists mostly of desert and semi-desert, it has very little natural vegetation of any kind. The far north around the southern coast

Mount Damavand is the highest mountain in Iran and the whole of the Middle East.

of the Caspian Sea has the heaviest rainfall of all and this has resulted in a Mediterranean-type evergreen forest.

These diverse geomorphological and bio-geographical characteristics determine the suitability of those lands between the Caspian Sea and the Persian Gulf for the support of human societies. This is what the early migrants discovered when they moved southwards during the second millennium BC, and the environmental conditions they encountered strongly influenced the nature of the societies which subsequently evolved in these areas.

The People

The land of Iran has been settled by human beings for many millennia. While primitive pastoralists lived around the mountains and on the more favourable parts of the plateaux, far more advanced societies were developing in the Mesopotamian basin on its western fringes. These were the first civilizations, town-dwelling people who evolved a sophisticated way of life, built fixed settlements, grew crops and developed the use of metals. On the boundary between the two in modern Khuzestan was one of the most advanced of these societies. These were the Elamites, who extended their territory from the plains into the mountains from

The Alborz mountains form a formidable barrier across northern Iran.

where they obtained metals and engaged in trade with the east. Their capital was Susa and this was the base from which they were able to gain control over a considerable part of Mesopotamia. They also developed strong trading relations with Sumer and other cities in the region. By the second millennium BC, Babylon had become the dominant city in Mesopotamia and it proceeded to create its own imperial state. Eventually the Elamites were themselves brought into the Mesopotamian political system and incorporated into the Babylonian Empire.

During the second millennium BC, these advanced urban civilizations of Mesopotamia were shaken by the arrival of new groups of people from the centre of Asia. This is known to history as the *Völkerwanderung* – the movement of peoples or Migration Period – that took place over a number of centuries. This extended migration was probably caused by changing physical and human conditions in their Asian homelands, including deterioration in the climate mixed with population pressures. These people came mainly from the steppes, the temperate grasslands that form a great belt across Eurasia from Eastern Europe to East Asia, and were primarily nomadic pastoralists and animal herders. Changes in climate conditions, which included diminishing rainfall, encouraged them to move away in the hope of finding better land. Such extended nomadic migrations created the conditions for tribal conflicts and eventually for more movements of people in search of new lands.

These migrants to the Middle East were in almost all ways very different from the native inhabitants. They have become generally referred to as Aryans, a word meaning noble birth in Sanskrit. The extensive migrations of the Aryans took them to a variety of places, but they moved in a generally southerly direction. The theory that they were all originally the same people is based on a number of factors, important among which is the discovery by linguists that there were great similarities in the languages spoken by the various branches of peoples who migrated into Europe, India and the Middle East.[1] The original homeland of the Aryans who moved to the south is now widely thought to have been the lands west of the Urals and north of the Black Sea, concentrated in present-day Ukraine and adjacent parts of southern Russia.[2]

Important among those who moved into the Middle East were the peoples who became known to history as the Medes and the Persians. Their most likely routes were either around the west or the east coasts of the Caspian Sea, where passes would have allowed them to penetrate through the mountains. It is known that large numbers first settled in the western parts of modern Iran around Lake Urmia. There they came into contact with the Assyrian Empire, a powerful and highly developed state centred in northern Mesopotamia. This state soon reduced the newcomers to a position of subjection. While the Persians moved away eastwards, the Medes consolidated themselves in the west and by the eighth century BC had established a strong state with its capital at Ecbatana on the edge of the plateau and just north of the Zagros mountains. The Medes then turned on their former overlords and in 612 BC, in alliance with the Babylonians, attacked Nineveh, the Assyrian capital, and within a few years had defeated the Assyrian Empire. Soon after this the Medes also gained ascendancy over the Persians, who were now settled well to the east. Persians had continued to move eastwards, well away from the major Middle Eastern conflict zone, and had settled in the area north of the main range of the Zagros. Known as Pars or Fars, by the early part of the first millennium BC this had become the main area of their settlement and the centre of the state that they proceeded to create. Although they continued to move widely, they came to regard Pars as their homeland and it always retained a very special place in their affections. From this came Persia, the name by which present-day Iran was known to the Europeans in earlier times.

Over time there came to be two centres of power in the lands that were occupied by these Persians. There was Pars itself, and another state called Anshan lying to the west. This division seems to have arisen from the fact that in the middle of the seventh century BC there had been two claimants to the throne and the failure of either to succeed in gaining it resulted in the creation of the two states. When this situation came to an end and the Persian lands were united, the new and more powerful state this created began to exercise a profound influence on the whole of the Middle East.

TWO

THE ACHAEMENID DYNASTY

The Achaemenid dynasty was established and given its name by Achaemenes, its eponymous ancestor, around 700 BC. The lands over which he had once ruled soon divided into the two separate kingdoms of Anshan and Parsa. It was not until 559 BC that Cyrus, the son of Cambyses I, ascended the thrones of both Anshan and Parsa and in so doing became the undisputed ruler of the Persian world. He was Cyrus II, the grandson of the first Cyrus, king of Anshan. In acknowledgement of his seminal role in the creation of the first Persian Empire, he has become known to history as Cyrus the Great.

Cyrus set about organizing the new state under his rule with a view to increasing its power and, in this way, gaining greater independence from its overlords, the Medes. It was not long before the Medes became aware of what was taking place under the new Persian king and alarm bells started ringing. They realized that they had to bring their vassal to heel without delay. It had to be made clear to Cyrus who really wielded the power in the Middle East. We learn from a contemporary source, the ancient cuneiform Babylonian Chronicles, that, 'King Astyages (of Media) called up his troops and marched against Cyrus, King of Anshan, in order to meet him in battle.'

The army of the Medes marched through Anshan and penetrated deep into Pars. There they confronted the forces of Cyrus at Pasargadae in the foothills of the Zagros mountains. They had come a long distance, while the Persians were on home territory. At Pasargadae the Persians conclusively defeated the Mede army and forced it to retreat. Cyrus pursued the Medes and besieged their capital, Ecbatana, forcing the city to surrender.

Seeing the way in which the geopolitical situation in the region was changing fast, Croesus, king of Lydia in western Anatolia, determined to take advantage of the instability. In 547 BC he invaded Media with the intention of replacing Mede domination with his own. Cyrus was certainly not prepared to allow this to happen and he moved westwards from Ecbatana, meeting the Lydian army at Pteria in the heart of Anatolia. Like the Medes before them, the Lydians were defeated and Cyrus continued to move westwards. As he had done with the Mede capital, he besieged Sardis, the Lydian capital, and this city also soon surrendered to the Persians. Following this surrender, the Lydian state collapsed and the whole of Anatolia was soon occupied by the Persians. Most significantly, this included the Ionian Greek cities on the eastern shore of the Aegean Sea, and these were also absorbed into the growing Achaemenid Empire. This was an event of particular historical importance because as a result the Greeks for the first time came into direct contact with the Persians. From that time on the confrontation between the Greeks and the Persians was to be a major occurrence in the history of the ancient world.

By this time Cyrus was in full imperial mode and the expansion of the new empire continued almost uninterrupted. In 541 BC he took his army northwards into Central Asia, which had remained a region of considerable turbulence. It was his aim to pacify the lands east of the Caspian Sea, a natural route southwards for the steppe nomads, and so to consolidate the vulnerable northern frontier. His army moved well to the north, occupying the huge lowland drained by the Oxus (Amu Darya) and Jaxartes (Syr Darya) rivers, which flow northwards into the Aral Sea. He established the frontier of his empire on the Jaxartes and there constructed fortifications for defence against the tribes to the north. This military foray was the first Persian incursion into that inland Mesopotamia known as Transoxiana, in which Persia was to be heavily involved in the future. It was to be one of the principal routes taking Persian influences into Asia.

Still bent on further conquests, Cyrus turned back westwards towards Babylon. This had long been the greatest city in southwest Asia and the chief centre of that urban civilization which had always been attracted to the inhabitants of the steppe lands to the north. Historically, Babylon had dominated Mesopotamia but had become increasingly unstable during the reign of its incompetent king Nabonidus and his son Bel-shar-usur (Belshazzar). In 540 BC Cyrus attacked the city and defeated the Babylonians at the battle of Opis. He then treated this great centre of urban civilization with great respect. Officials were allowed to keep their posts and Babylonian religious practices were allowed to continue. The Babylonian vassal states were also added to Cyrus's empire. These included the Phoenician cities in the eastern Mediterranean, which gave the Persians further access to sea power. A particularly significant gesture was that Cyrus ended the 'Babylonian Captivity' of the Israelites, who were allowed to return to their homeland and to rebuild their sacred temple in Jerusalem, which had been destroyed by the Babylonians.[1]

As a result of these conquests, within a quarter of a century Cyrus had transformed his small inheritance into an empire that stretched from the Mediterranean deep into Central Asia and from the Caspian Sea to the Persian Gulf. By this time it had become clear to him that endless conquest was not sufficient; it was necessary to have a system of government, in order to rule effectively the vast areas conquered. As a result of this, the empire was divided into provinces called satrapies, each governed by a governor, or satrap. According to the Greek historian Herodotus, eventually there would be twenty of these, most of them based on former vassal states of the empire. The other necessity was to establish a capital city from which the enormous empire would be ruled and its boundaries defended. In the early stages of conquest, Susa was chosen for this function. Chief city of the land of the Elamites, Susa was located on the western edge of the Zagros mountains, facing the great prize of Mesopotamia itself. As such it was a 'forward' capital, facing westwards, the main direction in which the empire was moving at this time.[2] It also had good communications and was chosen to be the terminus of the Persian Royal Road, which was intended to be the main axis of the empire and which initially stretched from Susa to Sardis. However, from Cyrus's point of view, Susa did have disadvantages. Most importantly, it was not in the historic Persian lands that held a special place in the hearts of the Persians. It was in Parsa that the Persians had first settled and it was there that the great victory over the Medes had taken place, signalling the beginning of the Persian journey to empire. Cyrus decided that Pasargadae, the place of the battlefield, should now be transformed into the place of government. There he embarked on the construction of his imperial residence, barracks to house the army and administrative buildings to house the agencies of government. As a result of this, two capitals came to share responsibility for the running of the empire, but it was Pasargadae that had the more important place in the affections of the Persians.

Despite the work involved in building a capital worthy of the achievements of the Persians, there were still pressing needs on the frontiers and Cyrus found it impossible to completely substitute his role of general for that of ruler. In 528 BC he was again on the frontier, this time in the north doing battle with the fierce nomadic tribes who lived there. It was in this conflict, in 530, that Cyrus was killed.[3] His body was returned to Parsa and laid to rest in Pasargadae, the site of his first great battle. From then on, the significance of Pasargadae to the Achaemenids was enhanced by the tomb of Cyrus the Great.

Cyrus's successor was his son, Cambyses II, who endeavoured to continue the policies of his father and extend the empire yet further. The main achievement of his brief six-year reign was the conquest of Egypt. This conquest took the Achaemenid Empire as far as Libya and it extended along the southern shores of the Mediterranean as far as the Cyrenaica peninsula. As a result of this, the empire became a Mediterranean as well as a Middle Eastern power and so inevitably came ever closer to the world of the Greeks. The city-states of this maritime people were by this time dominating the trade and the politics of the eastern Mediterranean and to them the Persians were very unwelcome intruders.

Following the early death of Cambyses and the absence of an heir, there were disputes over the succession. While in the

THE ACHAEMENID DYNASTY

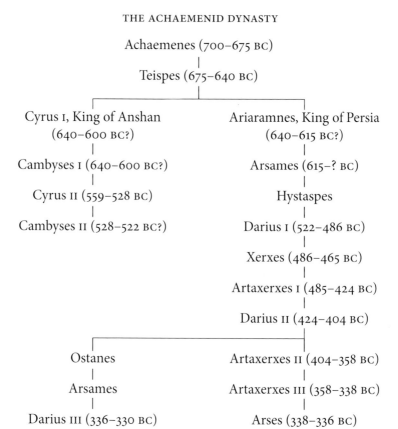

Achaemenes (700–675 BC)
|
Teispes (675–640 BC)

Cyrus I, King of Anshan (640–600 BC?)
|
Cambyses I (640–600 BC?)
|
Cyrus II (559–528 BC)
|
Cambyses II (528–522 BC?)

Ariaramnes, King of Persia (640–615 BC?)
|
Arsames (615–? BC)
|
Hystaspes
|
Darius I (522–486 BC)
|
Xerxes (486–465 BC)
|
Artaxerxes I (485–424 BC)
|
Darius II (424–404 BC)

Ostanes
|
Arsames
|
Darius III (336–330 BC)

Artaxerxes II (404–358 BC)
|
Artaxerxes III (358–338 BC)
|
Arses (338–336 BC)

early seventh century BC the kings of Anshan had succeeded to the throne of the united Persian kingdom, the succession now moved back to the branch that had ruled Pars. Darius, a descendant of Ariamnes and a distant cousin of Cambyses, became the Shahanshah, the Great King, and as Darius I he was to rule the empire for more than thirty years. Like Cyrus, Darius had a military background. He had been commander of an elite force known as the 'Ten Thousand Immortals' and had been closely involved with military operations on the frontiers. Much of the subsequent development of the empire was the work of Darius.

The uncertainties over the succession resulted in the outbreak of rebellions in Babylonia and Elam, but these were soon subdued. Darius then moved eastwards to the turbulent eastern frontier.

Defeating the Afghan tribes, the Persians invaded India and established a new frontier on the Indus river. The junction between the northern and eastern frontiers was secured by establishing control over the Hindu Kush, the huge knot of mountains located between Central Asia and the plains of northern India.

Having thus secured the eastern frontiers, Darius then turned westwards against the Greeks. The Ionian Greeks of Anatolia had been absorbed into the Persian Empire by Cyrus, but across the Aegean lay the major Greek city-states on the large peninsula lying between the Aegean and the Ionian seas. The largest and most important of these was Athens, and much of the Greek world was clustered around this city in a kind of unofficial and unstructured federation. These Greeks of the western Aegean encouraged the Ionian Greeks to assert their independence from the Persians and so to regain their historic liberties. This was another frontier that Darius was determined to stabilize and this necessitated moving ever deeper into the Mediterranean. In 513 BC his army crossed the Bosphorus on a floating bridge and embarked on the first invasion of Europe by an Asiatic power in historical times. This inaugurated a new phase in history. Herodotus, dubbed 'the father of history', asserted that the Persian army consisted of seven million men. While this was an example of Herodotus' notorious exaggeration, the army was certainly of a formidable size.[4] Thrace and Macedonia were occupied with little difficulty and this put the Greeks into a highly vulnerable position. Aid was sent to the Ionian Greeks in order to encourage them to rise up against their Persian overlords, and they were able to force a withdrawal of the bulk of the army back into Anatolia.

The Greeks of the western Aegean were now the last people in the ancient world to hold out against the Persian onslaught. In order for Persia to become the truly universal state of the western *oikoumene* it was necessary for this maritime people to be subjugated like all the others.[5] Darius decided to strike straight at the heart of the Greek world and this necessitated Persia becoming for the first time a sea as well as a land power. The maritime skills of the Phoenicians of the eastern Mediterranean were used and the ships were largely of Phoenician design.

In 490 BC a Persian army of approximately 25,000 men crossed the Aegean in 600 ships. They disembarked at Marathon on the coast of Attica, some 24 miles to the north of Athens. The army of the Athenians and their allies moved northwards to confront the Persians. The subsequent battle was a resounding victory for the Greeks, and the Persians had to escape back across the Aegean, having suffered considerable losses. For the first time since Cyrus defeated the Medes at Pasargadae, the Persians had themselves suffered a major defeat. Their proven strength as a land power was not matched by their attempts to become a sea power. The Greek victory proved that the Persians were not invincible.

While Darius, like his great predecessor, was much occupied with the stabilization of the frontiers, which inevitably meant the extension of the territory of the empire, he also found time to give attention to the internal affairs of his realm. It was Darius who gave Pasargadae, in the heart of Pars, its special significance and consolidated its position in the Persian mind by building the great tomb for Cyrus on the site of his first – and perhaps greatest – victory. As a result of this it became a place of pilgrimage and of imperial ceremony.

Cyrus himself had intended it to be his ceremonial capital and had begun to build there. However, the last thing Darius wanted was to be overshadowed by Cyrus, and from the outset he planned to have his own capital. He wanted his achievements to be seen as being quite separate and different from those of his great predecessor and needed a place to display the splendour of his own reign. This capital would have to be in Parsa and so relatively close to Pasargadae at the heart of the realm. Emphasizing this, the new city would be called Parsa. The Greeks subsequently Hellenized this and called it Persepolis, the name by which it has come to be known.

After the humiliating defeat by the Greeks at Marathon, Darius seems to have accepted the situation in the west. The Greeks of the western Aegean remained independent and the Persian dream of conquering Europe was abandoned. However, in 486 BC Darius was succeeded by his son Xerxes, who certainly did not share his father's acquiescence in this situation. While Darius had attempted

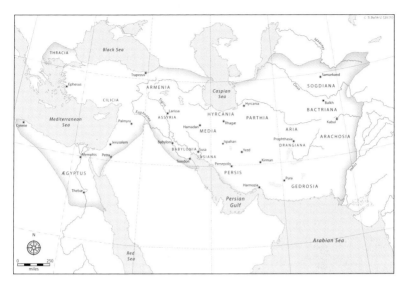

The Persian Empire at its greatest extent, 526 BC.

in most ways to follow the example of Cyrus as a benevolent and humane ruler, Xerxes was more prepared to use force to keep his subjects in order. A revolt in Babylonia was quelled with considerable brutality and Babylon was so badly damaged that it never fully recovered. This destruction of the richest city in the ancient world impoverished the whole empire.

The new Great King was determined that what today would probably be called the 'western question' had to be resolved. Herodotus attributed to him the pronouncement,

> We shall so extend the empire of Persia that its boundaries will be God's own sky, so that the sun will not look down upon any land beyond the boundaries of what is ours . . . I shall pass through Europe from end to end and make it one land.[6]

Presumably that one land would have been the Persian Empire, into which Europe would have been incorporated. Xerxes prepared for the next phase in the wars with the Greeks, and this time it was to entail the deployment of overwhelming land and sea power by the Persians. Xerxes planned that the army should take the easiest crossing into Europe via the Hellespont (the Dardanelles) while a Persian fleet was to cross the Aegean for the purpose of supplying and supporting the army.

In the spring of 480 BC Xerxes and his army crossed the Hellespont again, using a bridge of boats, and marched westwards through Thrace and Macedonia. Turning southwards into the peninsula, by August of that year they had reached Thermopylae where, despite showing great heroism, the Greek army was defeated. From there the Persians moved on and reached Athens itself. The city was poorly defended and its walls were inadequate to withstand attack. It soon surrendered and the heart of the Greek world was now in the hands of their greatest enemy. It seemed at this point as though Xerxes had achieved what his predecessor had failed to do, and he was poised to complete the long-desired conquest of Europe.

Yet the Greeks were by no means defeated. Athens was a maritime power and the Athenian leader Themistocles had stressed that the safety of the Greeks from the Persians could be ensured only by the construction of a powerful fleet by Athens and her allies. After the fall of the city, the Athenian fleet, together with ships sent by its allies, remained intact in the Straits of Salamis, and the Persian fleet was drawn into this narrow stretch of water. The two fleets clashed and the battle became one of hand-to-hand combat. The lightly armed Persians proved to be no match for the heavily armed Greek hoplites and the battle became a complete disaster for the Persians. By the time the battle came to an end there were very few Persian vessels left undamaged and the Persian losses were immense. (The Greek dramatist Aeschylus himself fought in this battle and later described what he had witnessed in his drama *The Persians*.) The Great King and his army who had watched from the shore were dismayed. At that point Xerxes lost his nerve and ordered an immediate retreat. The English military historian Geoffrey Regan expressed the opinion that the Persians had at first seen the battle as being a kind of sporting event, a grand spectacle to inaugurate the conquest of Greece and of Europe.[7] However, maritime combat was not a sport with which the Persians were at all familiar and there was to be no permanent conquest of Greece, let alone Europe.

In the maritime environment of the Mediterranean, land power proved to be no match for sea power. Regan compared the subsequent Persian retreat northwards from Athens to the Hellespont to Napoleon's retreat from Moscow. Likewise Salamis can be compared to Trafalgar, where the power dominant on land was no match for the maritime power at sea. As the great Persian army returned northwards it was harried by the Greeks and subject to disease and shortages of food. The army that arrived back in Asia was a sad shadow of the magnificent force that had set out earlier in the year, and the Persian fleet had been practically wiped out.

In the following year a Persian army of considerable size, which had been left behind with Greece in the hope of being able to resume the campaign, was conclusively defeated by the Athenians at Plataea. There were no further attempts by the Persians to complete their dominance over the ancient world by conquering Greece.

The Tomb of Cyrus the Great at Pasargadae.

Their European dream had come to an end. The reign of Xerxes was proving to be a disaster externally and internally and in 465 BC he was assassinated by one of his ministers. The Achaemenid Empire lasted for another 150 years and there were six more Great Kings, but the days of glory were already at an end.

The son and successor of Xerxes, Artaxerxes I (*r*. 465–424 BC), set the tone for the future. Following a revolt against him, he had all his brothers murdered and married his sister. This crime did little to stabilize the empire and further trouble on the frontiers was followed by the first losses of territory. The Greek city-states of Ionia on the eastern side of the Aegean became fully independent and moved completely into the Greek world.

Intrigue, corruption, feuds and murder now became the norms in court life. Artaxerxes III (*r*. 358–338 BC) seems to have murdered most of the royal family so as to remove any possible rivals to the throne, and he in turn was murdered by his chief minister. The political and moral decline continued unabated and the frontiers of the empire continued to shrink. Following the loss of Egypt and the defeat by the Greeks, Persia had virtually ceased to be a Mediterranean power and its influence in the ancient world continued to diminish.

The last Achaemenid king was Darius III, who ascended the throne in 336 BC following the death of Arses, who had been little more than a puppet king and like so many of his predecessors was murdered. Darius III was descended from Darius II – the great-grandson of Darius the Great – in another branch of the royal family, which had survived the spate of murders that had decimated the immediate succession. He made strenuous efforts to reassert the power of the monarchy, but by this time it was too late for any actions to save the Achaemenid dynasty. It is interesting that the final demise of the dynasty was brought about by the Greeks, the people who had prevented the Persians from becoming the empire of the ancient world and the dominant power in the *oikoumene*. While the Persians had failed to overcome the sea power of the Greeks, the latter overcame the land power of the Persians. More specifically, this huge reversal was brought about not by the Greeks themselves but by a people on the edge of the Hellenic world whose territory was minute by comparison with the vastness of the Persian Empire. These were the Macedonians, and the fall of the Achaemenid dynasty was accomplished by their king, Alexander, known to history as 'The Great'.

THREE

THE ACHIEVEMENTS
OF THE ACHAEMENIDS

The Achaemenid Empire was the first to achieve a dominant position over the greater part of the ancient world. In creating this universal state its rulers were faced with both problems and responsibilities. The main issue was how this great empire was to be maintained. This was achieved by the creation of an internal organization, which, as has been seen, was based on the satrapies – provinces – ruled by the satraps, or governors. Alongside this came the establishment of a legal system. Everybody except for the Shahanshah himself was subject to the law and this was designed to ensure the fair treatment of all. In one of his inscriptions in Susa, Darius asserts, 'My law, of that they are afraid, so that the stronger does not strike the weak, nor destroy [him].' In another inscription in Naqsh-i Rustam, Darius asserts that it is 'not my desire that the weak should have wrong done by the strong'. There was always the support of the god Ahuramazda in the establishment of order; the same inscription in Naqsh-i Rustam continues, 'Ahuramazda, when he saw this earth disturbed, after that bestowed it on me'. Darius then 'put it down in its place'. In the sense used here, 'to put it in its place' meant replacing chaos with order, and this was certainly one of the major achievements of the empire.

The conquered peoples were also treated in a humane manner. Like all subjects, they were protected by the laws, but additionally their own laws, cultures and religions were treated with respect. After his conquest of Babylon, Cyrus worshipped in the Temple of Marduk, and after his suppression of the revolt there Darius did the same. There was no attempt to convert the subject peoples to the religion of the conquerors. The conquered peoples were permitted, and even encouraged, to continue their own worship as they had before. One of the most notable examples of this was the freeing of the Jews from the so-called Babylonian Captivity and the rebuilding of the Temple in Jerusalem.

The system of government that Cyrus established and Darius consolidated can thus be considered to have been both liberal and enlightened. As a result of the freedoms they were given, most of the subject peoples became more contented and willing to accept Persian hegemony. Arnold Toynbee was of the opinion that the Achaemenid Empire actually developed many of the characteristics of a federal system, under overall Persian supervision.[1] Whether it could be called the first empire or the first federation, the political structure created by the Achaemenids succeeded in bringing order to the Middle East and enabled it to function as an organized whole for the best part of two centuries.

Another Persian achievement was success in creating what was perhaps the world's first common market. Old boundary restrictions were removed and as a result trade flourished throughout the region as it never had before. This led to considerable prosperity among its diverse peoples. The Phoenicians of the Levant coast, now within the Persian Empire, had been largely excluded from maritime trade by the Greeks. These Phoenicians now had the market of the entire Persian Empire at their disposal. Much of the Persian knowledge of ships and maritime activity actually came from the Phoenicians. Likewise, the Ionian Greeks of western Anatolia also benefited from this imperial common market and were less enthusiastic than their kinsfolk across the Aegean to regain their independence. The common language facilitating transactions was Aramaic, and this Syriac language was used widely by the merchant classes. Farsi, the language of the dynasty, became the language of government and administration throughout the empire. Commerce was further facilitated by the establishment of a common currency and a common system of weights and measures.

Above all, maximizing the benefits of the Persian common market also necessitated the construction of an efficient road system. The main axis of the empire was the Royal Road, which connected Sardis with Susa and Persepolis. Linked with this were other roads to the eastern Mediterranean coast, Mesopotamia, and the north and east. As well as for use by merchants, this road system was designed to ensure rapid communications across the empire for couriers and the imperial postal service. Herodotus was clearly highly impressed with the speed that was possible on these roads. He describes the couriers in some detail as follows:

> No mortal thing travels faster than these Persian couriers. The whole idea is a Persian invention, and works like this: riders are stationed along the road, equal in number to the number of days the journey takes – a man and a horse for each day. Nothing stops these couriers from covering their allotted stage in the quickest possible time – neither snow, rain, heat nor darkness. The first, at the end of his stage, passes the dispatch to the second, the second to the third, and so on along the line . . . the Persian word for this form of post is *aggareïon*.[2]

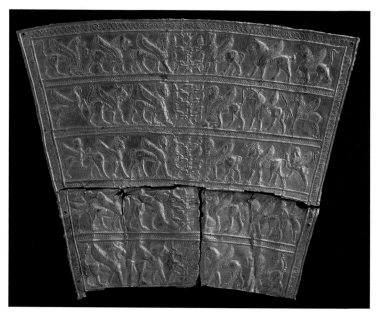

Gold plaque featuring winged creatures, said to be from Ziwiyeh, 7th century BC.

Frieze at Susa depicting palace guards.

The importance of trade is clearly demonstrated in the cuneiform inscriptions in Susa relating to the building of the royal palace there. According to these inscriptions the cedar wood was brought from Lebanon, while 'yaka' wood was brought from Gandhara. The gold came from Sardis and Bactria, and the blue precious stones (lapis lazuli) and the red (carnelian) from Sogdiana. Other precious stones were brought from Chorasmia, and silver and ebony from Egypt. The ivory was from Ethiopia and India while the ornamentation was the work of the Ionians. The Ionians worked the stone and the Medes and Egyptians worked the gold. The bricks were made by Babylonians. As a result of all these things, said Darius, 'In Susa a very excellent thing was ordered, a very excellent thing was (accomplished).'³ This splendid result is an example of the bringing together of the huge wealth of precious materials

This gold plaque of a winged lion-monster features heavy rings, suggesting it may have been worn on a leather belt. Achaemenid culture, Iran, *c.* 6th–4th century BC.

which the empire produced and the diverse craftsmen who were able to work with them.

The overall achievements of this first world empire are thus seen to have been considerable. They were able to push their opponents to the very peripheries of the known world and for the most part to secure the frontiers. Although the objective of Xerxes was never fully achieved – 'all lands' never actually became 'one land' – most of the immediate dangers to the hegemony of the Persians were removed. By their benign treatment of the subject peoples they created the conditions for internal peace and the consolidation of their power. The common market that came into existence also resulted in the creation of far greater wealth than had previously been possible in such a politically divided area. This all gave the Achaemenids the resources they needed to administer and defend the enormous territories that came under their rule. The creation of the universal state brought together a diversity of peoples and gave them peace and freedom from conflict. They were able to flourish in the cosmopolitan conditions and to a large extent came to accept their overlords in a way that was rare with future empires.

In the course of the two centuries of the Achaemenid dynasty, the Persians had changed from being pastoral nomads to living predominantly sedentary and urbanized lives. This brought about a surge in prosperity and a corresponding flourishing of arts and crafts. Objects were no longer fashioned simply for everyday use, but became valued as things of beauty and indicators of wealth. This process was enriched by the endless willingness of the Persians to borrow, learn and adapt the skills of various conquered peoples and also to use the materials obtained from all over the empire.

Buildings changed from being relatively simple wooden or mud-brick structures to being elaborate edifices in stone, such as those at Susa and Persepolis, designed to impress all who saw them. Craftsmen from all parts of the empire brought their own particular skills. Buildings were adorned with striking carvings and stuccowork. Glazed bricks were used to decorate internal walls. In the palace of Darius at Susa, one panel of such bricks shows a pair of winged lions with human heads, while another shows a procession of royal guards.

While there are few surviving examples of Achaemenid pottery, there is enough to show that here again they developed the skills already present in the conquered lands. What have survived are many fine examples of metalwork in the form of drinking vessels,

A cylinder seal and its print, Achaemenid period, Iran, *c.* 550–330 BC.

bowls and cylinder seals as well as military objects such as ivory and gold scabbards. Some of the finest examples of metalwork form part of the so-called Oxus treasure, found in the late nineteenth century in the northeast of the Achaemenid Empire near the borders of Tajikistan and Afghanistan. Among some artefacts from later periods, many objects that have been dated to the Achaemenid period were discovered. These include a heavy gold bracelet incorporating a pair of winged griffins, a golden jug with a lion-headed handle and several silver statuettes of human figures. Neil MacGregor chose a small model chariot in gold from this hoard as one of his '100 objects' of world history, and expertly shows its significance in the history of the Achaemenid Empire.[4]

The skill of patterned carpet weaving was also valued, again a 'refinement' from what were undoubtedly important domestic items in the tents of the early nomadic peoples. Jewellery was also highly prized. This gives an overall picture of a people enjoying the comforts and luxury of a civilized existence. This led the Greeks to admire the Persians on one hand but also to look down on them as having abandoned their frugal way of life and having become 'effeminate'.

The Persians' love of luxury even extended to the battlefield, and Herodotus frequently refers to the splendour of the Persian army and the lavishness of their equipment and way of life. He recounts that after the battle of Plataea, in which the Persians were defeated and forced to retreat from Greece, the Spartan leader Pausanias saw the splendour of the abandoned tent of Xerxes, with the table set in preparation for a feast. As a joke, he ordered an ordinary Spartan dinner to be prepared next to it. Summoning his commanders, he compared the two tables and laughingly commented on 'the folly of the Persians, who, living in this style, come to Greece to rob us of our poverty'.[5] Such luxury was perhaps the culmination of the Persian move from the simplicity of life on the steppes to the possibilities offered by the huge resources that the creation of the empire had placed at their disposal.

Perhaps the greatest achievement of the Achaemenids lay in the demonstration of what it was possible to become. Another of the inscriptions of Darius at Susa reads, 'By the favour of Ahuramazda I made everything beautiful.' The linking together

The gold chariot from the Oxus treasure.

of the utilitarian and the beautiful was certainly something the Persians did with great effect and they did it in many walks of life. The aim to make everything beautiful may not have been fully achieved but the fact that it was the objective of the Shahanshah pointed to the possibilities for the way in which empires could behave.

FOUR

Cyrus the Great in History and Legend

W hile there were many Great Kings during the period of the Achaemenid dynasty, Cyrus II, the founder of the empire, was the one who left the most indelible mark on the way in which the empire subsequently developed. However, while we know a great deal about its achievements, we know surprisingly little about its founder. In seeking to reach an understanding of Cyrus, history and legend come together and at times become virtually inextricable. Another complication is that much of what is known about him actually comes not from Persian sources but from others, most especially from the Greeks. Until the conquests by Alexander the Great, the Persians were the great foes of the Greeks and, largely because they were so different, the Greeks were in many ways fascinated by them and eventually found in them much that they respected and even admired.

What we know of Cyrus from Persian sources is very limited and comes almost entirely from cuneiform inscriptions on rocks and pillars. An inscription on a pillar of the palace at Pasargadae merely states cryptically, 'I am Cyrus the King, an Achaemenian.' Significantly, this inscription appears in Persian, Elamite and Babylonian.

The Cyrus Cylinder, which came from Babylon, contains an account of the way in which Cyrus entered the great city in triumph and allegedly was welcomed as a conqueror by its people. Most of the cuneiform inscriptions actually date from the reign of Darius and his successors.

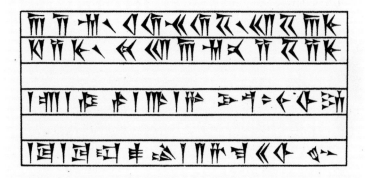

Cuneiform inscription on the royal palace of Cyrus the Great.

The most comprehensive and significant source of information about Cyrus is the Greek historian Herodotus, considered by Cicero to have been the father of history. Herodotus (*c.* 484–*c.* 424 BC) was born about half a century after the death of Cyrus and by the time he was writing, the reign was already history, albeit fairly recent. Herodotus was born in Halicarnassus in Ionia on the eastern coast of the Aegean and in view of this it is to be expected that he had a special interest in the great eastern empire into which the Ionian Greeks had by then been incorporated. However, partly on account of his obvious exaggeration of the numbers involved in battles, and the improbable tales he often told, others have seen Herodotus less as a historian than as a spinner of yarns. Longinus thought of him as being in the tradition of Homer and used the word *Homerikotatos* – almost Homeric – to describe his work. It seems evident that the history written by Herodotus was inextricably bound up with tales and legends.

In his great work the *Histories*, Herodotus wrote widely of the history of the world as known to the Greeks. Book One is devoted almost entirely to the Persians and to the Graeco-Persian Wars. As Herodotus was a Greek writing about these conflicts, one would expect considerable bias in favour of his own people, but that is by no means the case. Book One begins as follows:

> Herodotus of Halicarnassus here displays his inquiry, so that human achievements may not become forgotten in time, and

great and marvellous deeds – some displayed by Greeks, some by barbarians – may not be without their glory; and especially to show why the two peoples fought with one another.[1]

From the outset the approach is even-handed and the deeds and achievements of the 'barbarians' are frequently a source of admiration to the writer. The Persian view of history, and particularly the causes of the conflict with the Greeks, is given full weight.

Book One deals most particularly with the reign of Cyrus. Cyrus was said to be half Mede, since his father was Cambyses, king of Anshan, and his mother was Mandane, the daughter of Astyages, king of the Medes. As a result of a dream foretelling the triumph of the Persians, Astyages ordered that the child be put to death, but this was not carried out and he was secretly taken to the family of a herdsman in the countryside, where he was brought up. The truth of what had taken place was later discovered and Astyages allowed the young Cyrus to return to Cambyses in Anshan. When he succeeded his father, Cyrus turned on his Mede overlords and defeated them in the great battle of Pasargadae. Cyrus followed the remains of the Mede army back to their homeland, which the Persians then occupied. Thus began the foundation of the Persian Empire, which soon extended across the Middle East. Other later writers, such

The Cyrus Cylinder, citing a justification of the conquest of Babylon by Cyrus.

as the philosopher-historian Nicolaus of Damascus, a friend of Augustus, claimed that Cyrus was actually of very humble birth and that it was through his own innate qualities that he rose to importance in the court of Astyages. However, the dream predicting the victory of the Persians was also mentioned in Nicolaus' work. These legendary origins of the Great King are remarkably similar to those of other leaders, such as Moses.

It is from Herodotus that we get the picture of Cyrus being different from so many other great conquerors. There are many stories of his benevolence and of his kindness to the conquered peoples. Following the defeat of the Medes he spared Astyages and allowed him to live out his old age in peace. Following the defeat of the Lydians, their king, Croesus, was captured and sentenced to be burned to death on a funeral pyre. A last-minute change of heart by Cyrus is said to have saved the Lydian monarch from the flames.[2] Croesus subsequently became a member of the court of Cyrus and was present in the last battle fought by the great emperor. This was in Central Asia, east of the Caspian and near to what Herodotus called the Araxes river, where Cyrus was fighting against the Massagetae and their fierce warrior queen, Tomyris.[3] Tomyris advised Cyrus to return to his own lands, but Cyrus ignored her advice as he was still bent on expanding his empire northwards and deeper into the old Aryan lands. In a fierce battle near the Oxus river, Cyrus was killed. One has to conclude from Herodotus that a dominant characteristic of Cyrus was ambition, and it was this that eventually brought about his downfall. This was a version of the Greek *hybris* (arrogance), which for the Greeks was considered an inevitable path to catastrophe. This was all seen as being part of a divine plan to teach man humility. A later Latin verse talks of *fata* (fate), in finally ending the life of the conqueror of both the Medes and 'proud Babylon'.[4]

Despite the incorporation of stories and legends, the principal aim of Herodotus was to write history. Aeschylus (525–456 BC), on the other hand, was an Athenian playwright whose aim was to dramatize historical subjects.[5] As with Herodotus, his empathy with the Persians is very evident. His play *The Persians* centres on the great Persian defeat in the sea battle of Salamis that was crucial to the survival of the Greeks as a free and independent people. The Greek conflict with Persia was presented as being one of liberty versus despotism, yet the merits of the foe were always fully recognized. The Persians were seen in so many ways as being a noble people who behaved in a loyal and disciplined way, even in defeat. Of course, this battle took place half a century after the death of Cyrus, but the role of the Great King is recognized in a speech by Darius lamenting the Persian defeat at Salamis. In his lament for what had happened, Darius recounts the way in which the Persian Empire had arisen with the approbation of Zeus. Interestingly, the Greek god was used in this play, as the Zoroastrian god Ahuramazda, even if known to Aeschylus, would have meant little to a Greek audience. Zeus had given his authority for the establishment of a great empire, 'One man to wield his rod's authority over all Asia', beginning with Medus. In the succession of rulers:

> Third was Cyrus, fortunate, whose rule
> Brought peace to all: the Lydian people
> And the Phrygian he acquired,
> And marched his might against Ionia:
> No god resented him, for he was wise.[6]

Throughout history, it has been very unusual for an enemy to be presented in drama in so favourable a light, and it clearly demonstrates the respect the Greeks had for the Persians and especially for Cyrus himself.

The body of Cyrus was brought back to Parsa and buried at Pasargadae, the site of the great battle in which the Medes had been defeated. Later visitors to the site were moved by the lonely tomb of the great conqueror. Plutarch, in his biography of Alexander the Great, said how two centuries after the death of Cyrus, Alexander was moved (*empathe*) by the epitaph, which read: 'O man, whoever you are and from wherever you come . . . I am Cyrus founder of the Persian Empire. Begrudge me not, therefore, this little earth which covers my body.' Later visitors were equally impressed. 'The very venerable appearance of this ruin instantly awed me', wrote the Orientalist Claudius James Rich, who visited the tomb in the early nineteenth century, 'and I began to think that this in reality must be the tomb of the best, the most illustrious, and the most interesting of Oriental Sovereigns.'[7]

The Greek physician Ctesias spent some time at the royal court of Persia and became fluent in Persian. His story of Cyrus differs in many ways from that of Herodotus, including the assertion that there was no blood relationship between Cyrus and the royal house of the Medes, although after their defeat he had married the daughter of Astyages. Others have seen this as being an important contributing factor in the close relationship between the Persians and the Medes, which was one of the justifications for the Persian acquisition of empire. Ctesias also presents Cyrus as being less benign to his foes and asserts that he had actually connived in the death of Astyages.

In the middle of the fourth century BC, Xenophon wrote *Cyropaedia*, or *The Education of Cyrus*, a work that was later much commended by Cicero. Xenophon appears to have paid little attention to the historical record and to have concentrated on the positive aspects of Cyrus as a ruler. He saw Cyrus as being an example of the ideal prince and emphasized the qualities that were necessary to have made him so. Fundamentally, Cyrus was presented as having been a wise and humane ruler. He had a nobility and possessed a profound political philosophy. Xenophon's final verdict was that Cyrus had 'eclipsed all other monarchs, either before him or since'. In addition to this, Xenophon believed that Cyrus did not die violently but died as serenely as he had lived, 'with noble words of counsel on his lips'. Arthur Young considered this work to have been not so much history as 'a romance woven around an historical figure'. *The Education of Cyrus*, according to Young, 'is an extravagant tribute to a life the nobility of which has left many echoes in both Xenophon's time and subsequent eras'.[8] In many ways, Cyrus can be seen as having been the first example of the ideal ruler, an idea which later political thinkers were to develop, such as Machiavelli in *The Prince*.

As has been observed, another important example of the benevolence of Cyrus was in his treatment of the Jews following his conquest of Babylon. The Babylonian ruler Nebuchadnezzar had conquered Palestine and taken the captive Jews back to Babylon as slaves. This Babylonian Captivity was subsequently considered to have been one of the darkest periods in the whole of Jewish history. However, following the conquest of Babylon by Cyrus, the Jews were set free and allowed to return to their homeland. In the Book of Isaiah, the credit for this is given to Cyrus, who appears as a wise and benevolent ruler. Most significantly, in Isaiah, the Lord in His assertion on His supreme power gives Cyrus a place of honour among those who work for Him.

> He [Cyrus] is my shepherd, and shall perform all my pleasure; even saying to Jerusalem, Thou shalt be built; and to the Temple, Thy foundations shall be laid.
> Thus saith the Lord to his anointed, to Cyrus, whose right hand I have holden. (Isaiah 44:28–45:1)

Furthermore, and even more astonishing, according to Isaiah the Lord not only endorses the benevolence of Cyrus, but appears to express approval and support for his conquests. The Lord is holding Cyrus's right hand in order that he may 'subdue nations before him'. In the next verses of Isaiah, the support of the Lord for the Persian king appears to be absolute. The Lord says that in subduing the nations:

> I will loose the loins of kings, to open before him the two leaved gates; and the gates shall not be shut;
> I will go before thee and make the crooked places straight: I will break in pieces the gates of brass, and cut in sunder the bars of iron: And I will give thee the treasures of darkness, and hidden riches of secret places, that thou mayest know that I, the Lord, which call thee by thy name, am the God of Israel. (Isaiah 45:1–3)

In the Book of Ezra, there is more on the accomplishments of Cyrus and his close relationship to the Lord of Israel. Cyrus himself acknowledges that his great conquests are the work of the Lord:

> Thus saith Cyrus, king of Persia, The Lord God of heaven hath given me all the kingdoms of the earth; and he hath charged me to build him an house at Jerusalem, which is in Judah. (Ezra 1:2)

Ezra goes on to describe how Cyrus had given back the valuable ornaments that Nebuchadnezzar had stolen from the Temple. When the Temple was being rebuilt, the 'adversaries' of Judah attempted to frustrate the rebuilding and, although the rebuilding was slowed down, it went on 'for the Lord God of Israel, as king Cyrus the king of Persia hath commanded us'. According to Ezra 6, Cyrus took a special interest in the building of the temple, ensuring that it was built on solid foundations and its walls were high, and that the gold and silver vessels that had been stolen by Nebuchadnezzar be returned to their proper place.

Everything that is said about Cyrus in both Isaiah and Ezra is favourable. Besides his release of the captives and the rebuilding of the temple, the fact of his great conquests and his position as the king of 'all the kingdoms of the earth' is fully endorsed. It was an endorsement from the Lord God of Israel, who had been supporting him in all these things.

In Roman and post-Roman times, the adulation of Cyrus continued. Flavius Josephus in his *Jewish Antiquities* written in the first century AD asserted that Cyrus considered it his heaven-sent destiny to return the Jews to their homeland and to rebuild the Temple. To this end the necessary funds were provided. St Jerome in his commentary on Isaiah notes the reverence felt by the Jews for Cyrus. He was considered to be the one chosen by God to do His will. The rebuilding of the Temple at Jerusalem was begun during the reign of Cyrus but not finished until the reign of his successor, Darius. In the eleventh century, the monk Herva de Bourg-Dieu called Cyrus a 'pastor Dei' (shepherd of God) for all the good he had done to the Jewish people. A sixteenth-century edition of the *Jewish Antiquities* includes a magnificent miniature by the painter Jehan Foucquet entitled *The Clemency of Cyrus*. The Persian king is seated on his throne in some magnificence, receiving the petitions of the leaders of the Jewish people.

However, Josephus accepted that Cyrus died in the war with the Massagetae and was beheaded in front of their fierce queen Tomyris. Later writers emphasized the fate of Cyrus as being a lesson in the folly of ambition. Cyrus was attempting to extend his kingdom too far into areas inhabited by people whom he found it difficult or impossible to defeat. The historian Marcellinus writing in the fourth century AD also stresses this. Marcellinus was mainly interested in writing a history of the Roman Empire, but he looked back to the Persian Empire as being the forerunner of Rome. He expressed the opinion that what had brought down Cyrus was similar to what centuries later brought down Rome. Both St Augustine and St Ambrose were also deeply troubled by the fall of Rome and the implications of this for the destruction of the Christian world. To them, the fall of Rome was the fall of civilization and the coming of a time of chaos and destruction. In their attempts to understand history, both looked back to Cyrus, less as a model than as an example of that overweening ambition which they considered to be at the root of the fall of empires. Many of the subsequent Christian and pagan writers were most concerned with the tragedy of the fall of Cyrus and with the reasons for this. Boethius, in the early sixth century, wrote of the goddess of Fortune and the wheel on which human affairs turned. Dante puts Cyrus in Purgatory – mainly, it seems, because of the overweening ambition that had led him to disaster against Tomyris and the Massagetae.

It can be seen from all this that the medieval Christian writers were most inclined to use the story of the death of Cyrus to illustrate the premise that pride goes before a fall. The fate of Cyrus was nothing but the judgement of God on him for his ambition. There is very little in these writers about the virtues of the Persian king who had been extolled to such an extent by the ancient writers, notably Herodotus and Aeschylus.

A great deal of what was written by the medieval writers on the subject was also intended to help explain the fall of Rome, which was widely seen to have been a major catastrophe that left the world in chaos. They sought to generalize from this by attempting to understand the reasons for the fall of empires and in doing so they took a particular interest in Rome's great predecessor.

With the coming of the European Renaissance – the New Learning – the work of the ancient writers became once more available and this produced a further re-evaluation of Cyrus and the Persian Empire. The new editions of Herodotus and of Xenophon published in 1516 introduced Renaissance scholars to the more enlightened aspects of Cyrus's reign rather than his doom, which had been emphasized in the Middle Ages. Matteo Bandello (1480–1562), for example, relates a version of one of Xenophon's stories. The beautiful Babylonian Panthea was captured at the time of Cyrus's conquest of the city. As she was a prize of war, Cyrus sought to marry her, but out of respect for her unflinching devotion to her husband, Abradatas, Cyrus freed her and put her under his protection. The positive aspects of the story of Cyrus now became part of the knowledge that the Renaissance was revealing, and these revelations contributed to the better understanding of the pre-Christian world. Most importantly, Renaissance scholars wished to make a clean break with the theology of the Middle Ages, and going back to the pre-Christian world was for them the ideal way of accomplishing this.

Niccolò Machiavelli (1469–1527), who was deeply involved with the difficult relations of the city-states of the Italian peninsula, found Cyrus of considerable interest. In his most famous work, *Il Principe* (The Prince), he attempted to outline the qualities he considered necessary for the ideal ruler. The understanding of Herodotus and other ancient writers led him to examine Cyrus and his imperial ambitions. In his *Arte della guerra* (Art of War), Machiavelli examined the conflict between Cyrus and the Massagetae and the way in which the advice of Croesus, to advance into the territory of the Massagetae and to do battle with them there, was the main cause of the disaster that ensued. Machiavelli also attributes to Tomyris the stratagem of feigning retreat and leaving behind large quantities of food and drink, which is the opposite of the Herodotus story and suggests that Machiavelli may also have been using other sources.

In the 1430s the Englishman John Lydgate, a contemporary of Chaucer, wrote a treatise, the *Fall of Princes*, which includes Cyrus and discusses the ambition that caused his fall. Thus by no means

Georg Pencz, *Tomyris with the head of Cyrus, c.* 1550–50, engraving.

were all the Renaissance writers emphasizing Cyrus's virtues. His fall was put down to reasons of strategy and bad advice rather than the wrath of god as in medieval times. Paintings and tapestries of the life of Cyrus during this period also added to the vividness of the portrayal of the Persian king.

A seventeenth-century historical novel by Madeleine de Scudéry entitled *Artamène, ou le Grand Cyrus* (Artamene, or Cyrus the Great) drew a picture of an ideal romantic hero who would have fit well in the French court of Louis xiv. Contemporary tapestries of Cyrus dressed in the aristocratic costume of the period depicted the king as envisaged in Scudéry's novel. Spanish eighteenth-century tapestries continued this romantic tradition, but also stressed the political importance of Cyrus as a model ruler, with one such tapestry carrying the inscription, 'Sovereign Power under Justice and Freedom'.[9]

Arthur Young maintains that 'Cyrus the Great was a history-maker born into a myth-making age.'[10] The Cyrus of history has been largely hidden by the figure who represents a variety of imperial characteristics, from the honourable and noble to the overly ambitious. The fact is that throughout the ages Cyrus became whatever that age wanted him to be.

One can see how different ages drew their own picture of Cyrus that accorded with the ideas they wished him to represent. To the Greeks, Cyrus appeared as a largely benign figure of considerable historical importance. He emerges as a supreme ruler who acted in a benevolent fashion and whose rule was often compared favourably with the imperfections of the Athenian democracy. However, while the Greek writers were prepared to acknowledge the negative as well as the positive qualities of the Persian king, an entirely admirable picture is presented in the biblical texts. Cyrus, who in the Bible is said to have released the Jews from their captivity and even contributed to the rebuilding of the Temple, appears as an unblemished figure of good. The Lord announced that he has held the right hand of Cyrus and endorsed the way in which Cyrus had subdued the nations. In fact Cyrus is depicted as an agent of the biblical Lord, and Cyrus himself acknowledges the way in which he has been supported by the Lord throughout his work. This is very much similar to the way Cyrus's successor Darius stressed the role of the god Ahuramazda at every stage in the process of empire building.

The Roman writers were most interested in comparing this earlier empire with Rome, and later in using it to help explain the fall of the Roman Empire. While Cyrus was often seen in a positive light, his actions, like those of later rulers, inevitably led to catastrophe. The Christian writers of medieval times were most inclined to condemn Cyrus and they saw his fall as the consequence of pride and ambition. The fate of Cyrus was presented as a lesson to all who sought to follow a similar course. These theological writers were most concerned with the workings of the divine in human affairs, the road to success being to follow the course prescribed by the deity. Influenced no doubt by the fall of Rome, they ignored the biblical texts that had presented a very different picture of the Persian ruler. With the Renaissance, all this again changed and Cyrus once more became the example of the good and benign ruler, exercising 'sovereign power under justice and freedom'. The paintings and tapestries of the seventeenth and eighteenth centuries emphasized this, with the image of a magnificent and powerful ruler, in the best romantic tradition of the time.

Throughout the 2,500 years since the death of Cyrus, the ancient ruler has enjoyed the sobriquet 'the Great' and has been regarded as being a ruler of considerable historical significance. However, this significance has regularly oscillated between Cyrus as ideal and Cyrus as warning. As with the fusion of history and legend, the two have most often come together to present the ideal of the benevolent prince at the same time the pitfalls into which power can become ensnared. Yet it is the image of Cyrus as the great and benevolent ruler that eventually came to the fore. This was perhaps most simply stated by Aeschylus, who summed up Cyrus's reign in *The Persians* with the words, 'No god resented him, for he was wise'.

The question of the value of empire and imperialism, which began with the Greek views of Cyrus, was to continue into modern times. The Great King, in both history and legend, has remained throughout a figure of considerable interest and relevance. Despite the lack of real historical evidence on the subject, it is above all through the work of Cyrus that the legacy of the Achaemenid dynasty has been perpetuated. Throughout the ages the dynasty and its first ruler have continued to fascinate all who have attempted to examine the realities of this long-gone civilization and to understand what the lessons of its rise and fall can teach subsequent ages.

FIVE

PERSEPOLIS: CITY, THRONE AND POWER

ersepolis is one of the very earliest examples of a purpose-built imperial city. Here, city, throne and power were fused together in a massive display of the magnificence of the Persian Empire. The idea for such a centre of power evolved during the reigns of Cyrus II and his successor Darius I.

Early on Cyrus realized the importance of establishing a capital city from which the empire would be ruled, and, following his victories to the west, he returned to the Persian homeland of Pars and there embarked on the building of a great palace at Pasargadae. Called in Old Persian 'Pasragarda', meaning 'camp of the Persians', this had been an early gathering point for the nomadic Persian tribes. Having also been the site of the great victory over the Medes, it held a position of considerable importance for the Persians. It was the place where the Persians and their empire had originated and so it rapidly gained an aura of being a sacred space. It was subsequently chosen to become Cyrus's de facto capital.

With the death of Cyrus in 530 BC there was a struggle for the succession and, after the short reign of his son Cambyses II, the throne passed to another branch of the dynasty and Darius I ascended the throne as Great King. While Cyrus had established his capital at Pasargadae, Darius, at first uneasy on his throne, decided that a new purpose-built capital was necessary as a clear demonstration of his own power. The new capital was intended to be a symbol of his reign and so would distance him from his illustrious predecessor. However, when Pasargadae was chosen as the site for the splendid Tomb of Cyrus – built in white limestone

– this was to reinforce the city's position as the most sacred place for the Persians. Darius chose a location some 50 kilometres to the southwest for his new capital Parsa, which became known to the Greeks as Persepolis. It was to be Darius's greatest building project and by far the most important symbol of his power.

Persepolis is situated on the Marv-e Dasht plain and surrounded by high mountains. There appear to have been many reasons for choosing this particular site for the project, a number of them relating to Persian historical events and mythology. The tales of the early Persian kings were collected by the great Persian epic poet Ferdowsi in the *Shahnameh*, the 'Epic of the Kings', and the area around Persepolis was believed to have had associations with the mythical early kings of Persia. The most important of these was Jamshid, and Persepolis came to be familiarly known as Takht-e Jamshid, 'The Throne of Jamshid'.[1]

The area is also by tradition the home of Rustam, the great Persian hero best known in English through Matthew Arnold's mid-nineteenth-century poem 'Sohrab and Rustum'. The importance of the sun, and possibly sun worship, can also be seen in the fact that the eastern entrance of Persepolis has been aligned in

Charles Chipiez's 19th-century drawing of the city of Persepolis, which was built on a raised platform and surrounded by gardens. It proclaimed the wealth and power of the Great King.

accordance with the point at which the sun rises over the plain on the summer solstice.

As is most usually the case, in addition to these mythical origins, there were also more practical reasons for the selection of the site. The city is located deep in the outliers of the Zagros mountains at a height of 1,500 metres. This would have made it a cooler place for the court to reside than the low-lying land of Mesopotamia where Susa, the city in which the day-to-day running of the empire actually took place, was located. Since the Persians had come from the north, they would certainly have preferred this climate, and the landscape surrounding the city would also have been far more congenial to them. Furthermore, the site is in the valley of the Kor river, which would have provided a water supply for the population. As the population grew, ample water could also be brought down from the surrounding mountains using the intricate system of underground watercourses that the Persians invented (see Chapter Seven). The Kor followed a structural depression in the Zagros that is aligned from northwest to southeast, and this facilitated communication with Susa and other major centres of the empire. The great axis of communication of the empire was the Royal Road, which connected Sardis with Susa. This was later extended eastwards to Persepolis itself. Finally, the importance of the geology cannot be underestimated. The local limestone was easy to work and proved an ideal material for the great buildings and monuments of the city. Thus a powerful combination of mythological, historical and geographical factors combined to produce what must have been judged at the time to be the most appropriate site for the location of Darius's imperial capital.

Work on Persepolis commenced around 520 BC. The city was built on an immense platform that rises some 15 metres above the surrounding land. As well as providing stability for the foundations, this would have made the city visible from a greater distance and enhanced its effect on all those who approached. It was intended above all to be a demonstration of the power of the Shahanshah and of the empire over which he ruled. The main entrance to the city was accessed by a flight of stairs that were shallow enough to allow horses to mount. The whole city was clearly designed with

Guardian bull at the head of the Great Stairway (above), and Darius at the head of the Great Stairway of the palace at Persepolis (right).

ceremonial purposes very much in mind. Its architecture was derived from that of the conquered peoples, in particular the Assyrians and Babylonians, but it possessed a greater sophistication than either. The brutal ostentation of the Assyrians was softened by the Persian architects.[2] At the top of the Great Stairway, the Gate of All Nations led into the Apadana, the great hall where many of the ceremonies of state took place. Another, unfinished, gate on the same side of the platform leads to the Hall of the Hundred Columns. This was also used for many ceremonial purposes. In both of these halls at various times state business would have been conducted and the Great King would have received the homage of his subjects.

There was another massive building on the platform that housed the state treasury. Persepolis being the place where tribute was received, the stored wealth of the dynasty had to be safeguarded. The decoration of the Apadana centred on the twin bull capitals surmounting the pillars, also to be found elsewhere in the palace. Among the most significant carvings are those along the wall of the Great Stairway. Here bas-reliefs depict the subject peoples climbing the stairs bearing their annual tributes for the Great King. In many cases it is possible to make out from their dress and appearance, and from the gifts they are bearing, the lands from which they had travelled.

This is confirmed by what is written on the inscriptions found in and around the city. While on the gold tablet of Ariaramnes there was great emphasis on Persia and its virtues, by the time of Darius it was rule over the vast imperial possessions that was being justified. One such inscription in Persepolis reads:

> I am Darius, the Great King, the King of Kings, the King of countries, which (are) many, the son of Hystaspes, an Achaemenian.
>
> Darius the King says: by the favour of Ahuramazda these (are) the countries, which I acquired, with this Persian people, which had fear of me (and) bore me tribute – Elam, Media – Babylonia – Arabia – Assyria – Egypt – Armenia – Cappadocia – Sardis – the Ionians, those of the mainland, and those of the

sea – Sagartia – Parthia – Drangiana-Bactria – Sogdiana – Chorasmia – Sattagydia – Arachosia – India – Gandara – the Scythians – Maka.[3]

On the bas-reliefs the Elamites are bringing a snarling lioness, the Bactrians are bringing a two-humped camel, the Egyptians a bull and the Ethiopians elephant tusks. The Indians have axes and a donkey. The Armenians are shown holding a horse and a large vase and the Assyrians a bull and spears. Undoubtedly many of these things would have been symbolic, and the real tributes would be of gold and other precious metals, destined for the treasury.

The Medes are also depicted on the bas-reliefs. Although also subjects of the Persians, they were always accorded a privileged position and they were respected as the people who had made possible the great achievements of the Persians. The Persian relationship to the Medes was in this way similar to that of the Romans to the Greeks; they were the civilizers and mentors of the imperial people. On the Great Stairway, while the Medes had the honour of leading the procession they are also shown in the role of officials conducting the ceremony. Halfway up the Great Stairway on the

The Great Stairway at the palace of Persepolis.

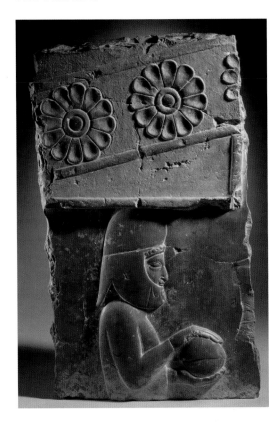

On this fragment from the ruins of Persepolis is a figure in Median dress holding a covered vessel, c. 500–450 BC.

wall behind the guards was the Faravahar, the winged sun disc and symbol of Ahuramazda.

W. H. Forbis considered this staircase to be 'perhaps the most engrossing socio-historical documentary ever put into stone' and 'a hand-chiselled filmstrip of obeisance to the emperor'.[4] Here at the ceremonial entrance to the capital was a perfect statement of imperialism in stone, and the Faravahar above it provided the divine justification for the whole imperial enterprise.

The two door-jambs of the Gate of All Nations at the top of the stairway are faced with the figures of the winged bull, bearded and crowned. Over the Gate is another bas-relief, of Ahuramazda. The level of the Apadana audience chamber was raised above that of the rest of the platform. There the winged god Ahuramazda is also

Eagle head atop a column capital at the entrance hall of the palace at Persepolis.

seen protecting the Throne of the Great King. It was in this hall that Darius and his successors would have received the homage of the representatives of the subject peoples and the tribute they brought.

The building work at Persepolis begun by Darius was later continued by his son Xerxes and grandson Artaxerxes. The whole area around the capital was the heart of Pars and because of its history and geography it became sacred space for the Persians. However, Pasargadae retained its special position as the site of the tomb of Cyrus the Great and so became a place of veneration for the founder of the imperial dynasty. The two cities were close enough to be linked both as twin symbols of the empire and as justifications for its existence. It was in Pasargadae rather than Persepolis that the elaborate coronation ceremonies of the Great Kings were conducted. However, other royal tombs were located in Persepolis or nearby. The tombs of the successors of Darius I, including Artaxerxes II and III, are on the hill immediately overlooking the city. Some 10 kilometres to the north of Persepolis is Naqsh-i Rustam, where the tombs of Darius and other successors were carved into the rock face.

On the tomb of Darius there is another inscription justifying the dominance of Persia. It includes the following words: 'Darius the King says: Ahuramazda, when he saw the earth disturbed, after that bestowed it on me; made me king. I am the King . . . Ahuramazda bore me aid until I did what has to be done.'[5] This constitutes one of the first clear statements of imperialism and the justification for it (of which more in Chapter Six). Thus within this relatively small area in the centre of Pars the Great Kings were crowned and buried, and the record of their achievements was hewn into the rock.

Jim Hicks saw Persepolis as having been 'a gigantic living monument – a conspicuous demonstration of the Persians rise from rude nomads to world masters, a colossally immodest salute to their own glory'.[6] It was certainly perhaps the most ambitious building project ever to have been undertaken at that time.

A Persian and a Mede depicted on the Great Stairway at the palace of Darius I.

The Persepolis capital region continued to retain its significance until the fall of the Persian Empire to the forces of Islam in the Battle of Nehawand in around AD 642. The Arabs swept through the ruins of the old capital and many of the carvings showing human figures were defaced. They were deemed to be un-Islamic, as was the old Zoroastrian religion itself. Persepolis soon disappeared beneath the dust and sand of the semi-desert which surrounded it and new centres of power were located elsewhere.

The poem 'Cities and Thrones and Powers' by Rudyard Kipling deals with the transitory nature of power. Power that at one time appears to be so absolute and permanent is inevitably destined to decline and disappear. Kipling's poem also captures the fact that the principal repository of such power is the city, and when a new power emerges it will also seek to display itself in a similar manner.[7]

While Persepolis remained a legendary capital, the evidence of its existence was lost in the sand for many centuries. It was rediscovered by travellers in the eighteenth century and excavated by archaeologists in modern times. In the twentieth century it was to have one more moment of quasi-imperial glory when Mohammad Reza Shah Pahlavi used it as the backdrop for one great – and final – celebration of his country's dynastic heritage.

Tomb of Darius I at Naqsh-i Rustam, the mountain range around 5 km north of Persepolis home to colossal rock-carved burial tombs of the Achaemenid rulers.

SIX

THUS SPAKE
ZARATHUSTRA:
RELIGION AND EMPIRE

T he Achaemenids and their achievements cannot be properly
evaluated without understanding the important part
played by their religion in these achievements. After the
Persians moved southwards from Central Asia into the Middle
East, where they came into contact with many other peoples, they
retained a strong feeling of racial and cultural identity. It was this
that held them together and was basic to the recognition that they
were different from those peoples already settled in the region. It
was also basic to their determination to throw off the shackles of
the Medes, their predecessors and overlords, and assert their independence. Despite these differences, they did have a great deal in
common with the other peoples of the region, who had migrated
southwards in much the same way at earlier times. Almost all these
people were of Indo-European stock, and this gave them many
racial, linguistic and wider cultural affinities.

However, in addition to their sense of identity, there was something else that was unique to the Persians. This was a religion with
which they became closely associated and which eventually under-
pinned their aspirations to power. This religion was Zoroastrianism,
which early on was adopted as the religion of the Achaemenid
dynasty and became deeply embedded in their political culture.
The central feature of this religion, and the one that gave it its
unique character at the time, was its monotheism. This set it apart
from the many polytheistic religions of the Middle East.

According to tradition, the religion was founded by the sage
Zarathustra, who was known to the Greeks as Zoroaster. He is

generally believed to have come from eastern Persia, or possibly from the Afghanistan borderlands around 1200 BC.[1] He had been most certainly a priest of a pre-existing polytheistic religion, but at some stage in his life he changed and began to preach monotheism. The religion itself appears to have taken hold around the sixth century BC. Its precepts are contained in the Avesta, the holy scriptures, some of which – the Gathas – are songs believed to go back to the time of Zarathustra himself. The Avestan texts were originally handed down orally and changes must inevitably have taken place over time. However, the basic beliefs of the religion were retained throughout the period of the Achaemenids.

The Zoroastrian god was Ahuramazda. He was the 'Wise One', the supreme being and creator of the universe. In this universe there are two opposing forces – Spenta Mainyu and Angra Mainyu. The former is the Good Spirit, based on truth, while the latter is the Evil Spirit, based on falsehood.[2] Asha is Goodness and Truth, while Druj is Evil and the Lie. There is thus an ethical dualism and human beings have the responsibility to choose between the two. In this way the religion also incorporates free will, which marks a radical departure from the polytheism that preceded it. While Zarathustra was very much against any remnants of polytheism being left in his new religion, some polytheistic elements did survive and came to be incorporated into it. Zarathustra himself taught that there are six Amesha Spentas, or Beneficent Immortals: Good Thought, Best Truth, Desirable Power, Great Devotion, Wholeness and Immortality. Ahuramazda was referred to as being the 'father' of these immortals. Not exactly gods, they were ideals or principles that were inherently part of the religion and its full expression.

In Zoroastrianism, truth was associated with physical purity, and this is represented by Atar (or Adur), fire. This was kept as an eternal flame in the fire temples in which Atar was venerated. The fire ceremonies that took place involved purification rites. The priests of the religion were the Magi, who are believed to have originally been the priestly caste of the Medes, and if so are another of the many borrowings made by the Persians from their former overlords. It is thought that they probably had the same origins as the Brahmin priestly caste in India. They were in charge of the fire temples and the ceremonies associated with them. They were also in charge of the disposal of the dead, which took place on the *dakhma*, or Tower of Silence. On these structures, vultures awaited the arrival of the corpses and they picked the flesh from the bones until the soul had departed the body, in a so-called 'sky burial'.

Zoroastrianism held out the prospect of a future age in which perfect human beings would exist. There would be a final battle, very much like Armageddon, in which Druj would be defeated and Angra Mainyu would be annihilated. This is also associated with a form of resurrection from which the worthy human beings, those who had followed Spenta Mainyu, would become immortal.

In time, more elements of polytheism seeped back in when they were deemed to be *yazata*, or worthy of worship. These included the Sun, the Moon, Rain and the Wind. In this way many gods were subordinate to the one god, a belief system with distinct similarities to the Indian Hindu tradition. The Sun god Mithra also possessed many of the characteristics of the early Aryan god Indra. Mithra came to be associated with the maintenance of law and with bull sacrifice.[3] The holy mountain of these gods was Mount Alborz in northern Persia and, as with the Hindu gods in the Himalayas, this accorded with the northern origins of the early Persians, their polytheism and the gods they brought with them. The persistence of these early gods made Zoroastrianism, in the words of Roman Ghirshman, an archaeologist who specialized in ancient Iran, 'an imperfect monotheism'.[4]

Zoroastrianism became the dynastic religion of the Achaemenids at a very early stage in the dynasty's existence, and at virtually the same time it became the official religion of the state. Evidence for the Zoroastrian belief is found in the many cuneiform rock inscriptions that have been discovered in various parts of Pars. The earliest such inscriptions are on gold tablets discovered by archaeologists in the 1920s. One of these purports to date from the reign of the Achaemenid king Ariaramnes, who reigned over Anshan during the second half of the seventh century. The translation of this tablet is as follows:

Ariaramnes, the Great King, the King of Kings, the King in Persia,

The son of Teispes the King, the grandson of Achaemenes.

Ariaramnes the King says: This country Persia which I hold, which is possessed of good horses, good men, on me the great God Ahuramazda bestowed [it]. By the favour of Ahuramazda I am the King [in] this country.

Ariaramnes the King say: May Ahuramazda bear me aid.[5]

Another gold tablet from the reign of Arsames, the son of Ariaramnes, expresses similar sentiments and also claims that 'He [Ahuramazda] bestowed on me the country of Persia.' Arsames then goes on to implore: 'May Ahuramazda preserve me and my royal house, and may he preserve this country, which I hold.'

While these gold tablets date from a time before the establishment of the empire, from then on religion and empire progressed in tandem. To use modern terminology, State and Church were fused and acted as one in the development of the empire. This close link was maintained throughout the whole period of the dynasty.

For the ancient Persians, Zoroastrianism provided the moral justification for their actions and in particular for the creation of the pre-eminent state in the Middle East. Central to this was the conviction that the Shahanshah, the King of Kings, held his empire in trust from Ahuramazda. The empire was the earthly representation of Asha (Truth, Goodness) and in its battles it fought against Druj (the Lie). Those whom the Achaemenids fought against, and those who rebelled against their authority, were referred to as 'liars'. The pursuit of Asha was thus considered to lead to a proper order, while Druj inevitably led to disorder and misery.

On the fire temples and royal palaces, Ahuramazda was represented as the Faravahar, the winged sun disc that decorated the walls of the palaces of Persepolis. Sometimes the god was also depicted in the form of a human figure with wings. The Shahanshah worshipped Ahuramazda as represented by the Faravahar in the fire temples, and there sought divine guidance and support for his actions. It was this interaction with the god that gave the king his own special qualities and so justified the supreme power

Ahuramazda as a winged figure. Relief carving in the Apadana, Persepolis, *c.* 500 BC.

accorded to him. An inscription in Susa asserts that Ahuramazda 'made Darius king, the one king among many [kings] the one commander among many [commanders]'. This made it clear that it was Ahuramazda who had given the Achaemenid dynasty its unique role in the world.

The Achaemenid kings, in particular Darius, left many inscriptions, most of them as rock carvings in the cuneiform script. While these tell us a great deal about the kings themselves and their activities, they tell us even more about the importance to them of the Zoroastrian religion. The support of Ahuramazda was an essential feature of everything that was done. After his invasion of Babylon, Darius acknowledged that

> Ahuramazda bore me aid, by the favour of Ahuramazda we crossed the Tigris. There I severely defeated that army which was Nidintu-Bel's. After that Nidintu-Bel, with a few horsemen, fled [and] went off to Babylon. After that I went off to Babylon. By the favour of Ahuramazda I both seized Babylon and I seized that Nidintu-Bel. After that I killed that Nidintu-Bel in Babylon.[6]

'By the favour of Ahuramazda' and 'Ahuramazda bore me aid' are recurring themes in the battles that Darius fought and this provided both the justification (favour) and the means (aid) for the achievement and retention of Persian imperial power. Always the command of Ahuramazda was: 'Do not leave the right path.' This 'right path' was, of course, that pursued by the Achaemenid dynasty, and opposition to it was 'the wrong path', or the path of evil. Darius asserts, 'I am the friend of right. I am not the friend of wrong . . . what [is] right, that [is] my desire.' As a result the Achaemenid imperial achievement was founded on the firm belief that their god guided their actions and so ensured their success. In order that this happy situation should continue, Darius always gave the assurance: 'I worshipped Ahuramazda.'

The actions of the Achaemenid kings were thus always presented as being motivated by the Spenta Mainyu, as they fought relentlessly against the Angra Mainyu. This was used to explain the rise of a small and relatively poor people, formerly pastoral nomads in the steppes of Asia, to a position of dominance over the ancient civilizations of the Middle East. Their certainty that what they

Darius I, overlooked by Ahuramazda, depicted on a rock relief at Mount Behistun, Iran, with cuneiform inscriptions.

were doing was right was founded on the firm belief that they had the authority of the universal god Ahuramazda, who was protecting them and guiding them along the right path.

'Thus Spake Zarathustra', the title of this chapter, is taken from the title of the famous book written by the German philosopher Friedrich Nietzsche from 1883 to 1885. In this book he showed himself to be a fierce critic of morality, especially the Christian morality of that time. Nietzsche was haunted by what he called 'ethical dualism', and his main aim was to pass beyond good and evil to what he considered to be higher ideas.[7] Zoroastrianism had been the first Middle Eastern religion to postulate the existence of good and evil and to emphasize the necessity of taking the side of good. For Nietzsche this was therefore the religion that had introduced something of which he thoroughly disapproved. However, it has been seen that the Achaemenids took a totally different view and saw in that religion the justification for their empire and for the way the empire should ideally be ruled. The way in which Zarathustra 'spake' was viewed in another entirely different way by twentieth-century Fascist states, such as the German Third Reich, which used the ideas of Nietzsche to justify their own barbarous conduct. Unfortunately the empire of the Persians was not often the model for how subsequent empires behaved.

SEVEN

PARADISE GAINED

The Indo-European peoples of Central Asia were nomadic pastoralists and when they migrated away from the steppe grasslands at the heart of the continent they brought their animals and their pastoral way of life with them. They encountered the sedentary urban civilizations of the great river valleys and were soon influenced by this new and unfamiliar world, and their own way of life began to change. However, as a result of the fact that the various Asiatic tribes migrated into what were geographically very diverse regions, they encountered a great variety of new terrains and types of land. As a result there were considerable differences among the peoples in their responses to these new environments.

The Aryans who moved southwards into the Indian subcontinent towards the end of the second millennium BC arrived at the great rivers of the Indo-Gangetic plain and there came into contact with the civilizations that had long been established around these rivers.[1] The waters from the Indus and the Ganges and their tributaries, together with the soils produced by the sedimentary material they brought down, were able to sustain rich agricultural lands producing an abundance of foodstuffs and other agricultural products. This diverse agriculture supplied the needs of the great cities of the urban civilizations of northern India. While the pastoral lifestyle of the Aryans did not fit well into this agricultural economy, the cattle they brought with them were cherished symbols of their earlier life in the dry steppes. The cow was closely associated with the legends of their nomadic past in the heart of Asia and in time the worship of the sacred cow became a central feature of their polytheistic Hindu religion.

The experience of those Indo-European peoples who migrated into the Middle East was in many ways similar. There they arrived at the two great rivers, the Tigris and Euphrates, and encountered the urban civilization that had arisen around them. This civilization was dominated by the great city of Babylon, one of the world's earliest cities, which dated back to the third millennium BC. This had been for much of its history both the political and the economic heart of Mesopotamia, the 'Land Between the Rivers'. However, by the time the Persians were migrating southwards at around the beginning of the first millennium BC, the region had already become overcrowded with other migrants. As has been observed, the powerful Assyrian empire dominated much of the west while the Medes had created their own strong state in the centre. Others, such as the Lydians in Anatolia and the Elamites south of the Zagros mountains, had also carved out their own powerful states.

Faced with this stiff competition for land, the Persians were at first denied access to the more productive areas in the west of the region. Moving southwards they crossed the dry plateau country between the Alborz and the Zagros mountains. The eastern flanks of this plateau are desert and semi-desert and the low rainfall is accompanied by very high summer temperatures. In the northern foothills of the Zagros mountains the Persians found at least some grazing for their animals and were able to establish themselves on the fringes of the more settled lands to the west. By the seventh century BC they had organized themselves into two separate but adjacent states, Anshan in the west and Pars – or Fars – in the east. The leading families of the two states were both descended from Achaemenes, founder of the Achaemenid dynasty, and there was much internecine rivalry between them.

Since the area into which they migrated was largely dry and unproductive it must initially have been even less attractive to these pastoralists than the steppe grasslands of Central Asia, which they had left behind in search of better lands. The steppe, and even the adjacent dry steppe or semi-desert to the south, had usually provided sufficient grazing for the animals, but this was by no means always the case in the lands into which they now moved. However, in the Zagros mountains themselves the precipitation was considerably higher and the melting of the snow produced abundant water in the spring. The existence of these geographical conditions led to the idea of irrigating the dry lands by taking water from the mountains and feeding it down into the plains. Of course, irrigation was by no means a new idea and it had been from the outset an essential feature of the agriculture of the urban civilizations of the river valleys. Mesopotamia's wealth had to a large extent been based on the knowledge and use of irrigation techniques. It was new, however, when used in the desert and semi-desert of the plateau. A major problem with irrigation in this area was the great distance the water had to be brought, combined with the extreme heat in summer of the dry lands through which it flowed. This resulted in substantial water loss into the ground and high levels of evaporation. If open watercourses or river diversions were used, the greater part of the mountain water would be lost well before it reached the grazing lands lower down. In natural circumstances, the rivers flowing from the mountains onto the plateau soon dry up on the plateau itself and very little of the water from the eastern Zagros mountains ever reaches the sea.

The problem of water supply was solved by something that all the evidence points to having been a Persian invention – the conduits known as *qanats*. It seems likely that the Persians invented and perfected this technology some time between the tenth and eighth centuries BC.[2] These were underground channels excavated from the mountains down into the lower lands and usually covered over with large stone slabs in order to protect the water from the heat. In some cases these were at a considerable depth below the surface, while in others, particularly in the higher land, they were just below the surface. These conduits proved to be an excellent method for transporting the water with very little loss and this meant that it was possible for otherwise unproductive land to be brought into use. Of course, initially the cultivation of crops was not something the pastoralist Persians would have known much about and the water would initially have been used mainly for their animals and, where possible, to improve the grassland. However, they soon learned about agriculture from the other peoples of the Middle East, in particular their neighbours the Medes who, as has been seen, were in so many ways the mentors of the Persians.

The Persians clearly found these irrigation techniques to be of considerable value for watering their animals, and also began early on to experiment with the growing of a variety of plants. In doing this they aimed to produce what was useful to them as food and, when they had done this, what would improve and beautify their harsh environment. In this way the useful and the beautiful were grown together in the artificially improved conditions. Thus while they grew flowers and trees to beautify their environment, they also grew fruits and vegetables. It was soon discovered that the high temperatures on the plateau during the summer months, together with the water brought down from the mountains in the qanats, produced ideal conditions for a wide range of cultivated plants.

However, while this was so, the heat that was good for cultivation was considerably less welcome to the human beings who worked the land. In order to deal with this, trees and bushes were planted to give cover, making the working and inhabited areas cooler. As with farmlands in many other parts of the world, the growing of trees around settlements proved to be highly beneficial in many ways. According to Ronald King, this would have been the origin of 'the classic Persian garden'.[3] The trees provided shade and protection and cooled the air to make life altogether more pleasant than it could be in the surrounding desert and semi-desert lands.

In order to use the precious water efficiently, relatively small areas were at first cultivated in this way, and from this comes the idea of the 'garden' rather than the farm. This was a huge contrast to the vast grasslands that the Persians would have been accustomed to in their earlier pastoral nomadic life, and this must have stimulated them even more to pursue their new techniques. The cultivated area would also have been walled in, to protect what was within from the harsh, dry environment outside. The evidence reveals that the water flowing down from the mountains in the underground qanats would have been stored in large tanks to ensure a constant supply throughout the year. When the water was released it would have taken the form of watercourses flowing through the cultivated enclosure. These would have had the dual function of both irrigating the enclosed land and, given their geometrical shapes, making the whole garden a more aesthetically pleasing environment. In this way the Persian garden developed into an art form.

This Persian creation in the midst of desert and semi-desert lands was the 'paradise' that became so central a feature of their lives. The Old Persian word *pairidaēza* means an enclosed park or pleasure ground. This was something that first came into being in the lands to which the Persians had migrated around the northern flanks of the Zagros. Since the whole concept dates from soon after the initial migration, the word would probably have originated at around this time.[4] According to King, it signified a warm and verdant 'in between' land, 'where sun and shade are equal and pleasant waters flow'. This artificially produced temperate environment was totally different to those extremes characterizing most of the Middle East. The enclosure of this precious space would then have been of considerable importance. As another writer put it, in the ancient Middle East,

Happiness was associated with enclosures rather than open spaces . . . for deserts and hills, the wind and the sun, were generally too harsh to man. When he thought of a pleasant

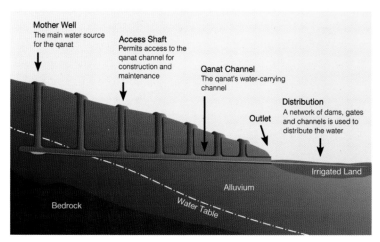

Diagram showing how water is carried along a qanat.

place he thought of an oasis or garden, where he could relax in the shade with ample water and fruit.[5]

The inadequacy of the natural environment into which the Persians had moved was thus completely transformed by the invention of the qanat. By its invention, it had been possible to create that 'pleasant place . . . with ample water and fruit'.

There is evidence that knowledge of the existence of the Persian *pairidaēza* was well established by the sixth century BC. Xenophon in the *Oeconomicus* tells how a Greek envoy was taken by Cyrus to admire his *pairidaēza* at Sardis, the old Phrygian capital. Cyrus took great pride in such gardens and seems to have found the time, among his many other activities, to be involved with the planning and even the planting.[6]

Among the most famous of the Middle Eastern gardens were the Hanging Gardens of Babylon, one of the Seven Wonders of the Ancient World. There are many accounts of their origins, probably the most widely believed being that they were constructed by Nebuchadnezzar II for his wife, who came from Media and missed its landscape of hills and streams. There is also the strong probability that they took their inspiration from the parks and gardens in the Assyrian capital, Nineveh. Interestingly, Diodorus Siculus, writing in the first century BC, has a different story. He maintains that they were actually built and laid out by Cyrus after his conquest of Babylon. According to Diodorus:

> The Hanging Garden of Babylon was not built by Semiramus who founded the city, but by a later prince called Cyrus, who, for the sake of a courtesan, who, being a Persian . . . desired the king, by an artificial plantation, to imitate the land in Persia. This garden was 100 feet long by 100 wide and built up in tiers so that it resembled a theatre . . . The highest gallery contained conduits for the water which was raised by pumps in great abundance from the river.[7]

When the German archaeologist Robert Koldewey was excavating at Babylon in the early twentieth century, he found evidence to suggest that the account of Diodorus Siculus was, in fact, surprisingly accurate.

As has been observed, the Greeks of the time were well aware of the Persian *pairidaēza*, which they saw as being another of the many positive achievements of their great but much admired opponent. Xenophon reports a dialogue of Socrates on the subject; according to the philosopher, the king of Persia was very much involved in gardens and gardening:

> In whatever province he resides, and wherever he travels, he takes care that there may be gardens, such as are called *paradeisoi,* stocked with everything good and valuable that the soil will produce; and that in these gardens he himself spends the greater part of his time.[8]

The historical and archaeological evidence reveals that while the Tomb of Cyrus now appears stark and solitary in the dry and uncompromising landscape of Pasargadae, this had not been the case during the Achaemenid period itself. It appears that at the time of the visit of Alexander the Great, following his victory over the Persians, the tomb was sheltered by a larger structure and was surrounded by beautiful gardens with many trees. Archaeological excavations have revealed that there were qanats around the whole area and that supplies of water were being brought down from the northern slopes of the Zagros mountains.

From the outset it had been necessary for the Persians to do something to improve their land if their great migration from Central Asia was to be at all worthwhile. Neither the bare and rocky mountains nor the desert and semi-desert below were of great attraction for human settlement but the bringing of water from the one to the other produced conditions that could hardly have been bettered. It was the protection of the cultivated land from the hot, dry plateau afforded by trees and walls that then enabled the *pairidaēza* to flourish. When these were laid out to surround villages and towns and the great palaces of the kings they created an integrated human landscape of buildings and gardens. Its huge contrast with the bare land outside would have made this landscape even more astonishing to visitors. Gardens of this sort would certainly have surrounded Persepolis and added greatly to the beauty, impressiveness and sense of power of the ceremonial capital of the Achaemenids.

There was no 'paradise lost' for the Persians, since they had migrated from an environment that was becoming ever more challenging. The paradise they 'found' was something that they themselves created, and it was eventually to become one of their most impressive legacies.

While the Persian paradise later became transformed into a religious idea in the Christian world, Persian Islamic writers have maintained that it also had a role in Zoroastrianism. In Ferdowsi's *Shahnameh*, the religious idea of paradise is very much present. Ferdowsi describes how the prophet Zoroaster created a paradise:

> He reared throughout the realm a tree with beautiful foliage,
> and men rested beneath its branches.
> and whoever ate of its leaves became learned,
> in all that regards the life to come,
> But whoever ate of its branches
> Became perfect in wisdom and faith.[9]

It was the translation of the Persian *pairidaēza* into its Greek form *paradeisoi* that first introduced the word to the Greek and later the European world. The Septuagint translators of the Bible in Alexandria used the word as a synonym for the Garden of Eden and early Christian writers later used it as synonymous with Heaven. The water for the Persian garden, after being stored in tanks, was usually separated into four parts, thus dividing the garden into four separate spaces. Remarkably, this was replicated in the description of the Garden of Eden where, according to the biblical text, 'a river went out of Eden to water the garden, and from thence it was parted, and became into four heads' (Genesis 2:10). It has even been suggested that the resemblance is so close that the layout of the Persian garden may have been something that the Jews observed during the Babylonian Captivity.

A 19th-century reproduction of the Hereford *Mappa Mundi*. Paradise with its rivers is in the east (top) and Babylon is located beneath it. Jerusalem is at the centre of the world.

The concept of paradise continued on into the Middle Ages, but it became transformed into an earthly paradise open only to the virtuous. While the Christian writers of this time saw Cyrus as being symbolic of the way in which emperors destroy their creations by being too ambitious for ever more conquests, they nevertheless took the idea of the Persian garden as symbolic of the place of perfection and they made it an essential part of the Christian story.

This can all be seen very clearly by an examination of the *mappae mundi*, the world maps produced in medieval Europe.

These are essentially idealized representations of the world as it was envisaged at the time. In one of the best-known of these – the Hereford *Mappa Mundi*, dating from the thirteenth century – Paradise is an island in the east, which is at the top of the map. It has four rivers flowing through it and a tree growing in the middle of them. This is the Tree of Life, and the tale of Adam and Eve takes place in this paradise. (They are, of course, eventually expelled from it because of their transgressions.) The picture is completed in the Hereford map with Paradise surrounded by a wall. The resemblance between this Christian Paradise and that of the Persians is so close that the influence of the *pairidaēza* is very obvious. Not far below it on the map is Babylon, complete with the Tower of Babel, which is, not surprisingly, seen as being the centre of iniquity.

In this and many other ways, the idea of paradise as originated by the Persians was taken up by medieval Christianity. Cyrus, the great lover of gardens, may have been reviled by Christians for his 'restless ambition', but the paradise he had created, and was said to love so much, was still considered to be an earthly ideal.

The Christian ideal of how humanity should behave and the moral code to which human beings should adhere bore certain resemblances to the ideals of the Achaemenids. They held to the firm belief that in building their empire they were engaged in doing the work of Ahuramazda (God) and that what they did was firmly based on Spenta Mainyu (Good Spirit) and Asha (Goodness).

The invention of the *pairidaēza* was certainly one of the Achaemenids' most important achievements, and the beauty of what they created became closely associated with their ideal of goodness. This then became an enduring part of the Achaemenid legacy, and its incorporation into later religious and other ideals was a demonstration of its perceived uniqueness and value well after the ancient empire had passed into history.

The qanats possessed two parallel functions. They enabled the emergence of beauty in what would otherwise have been barren ugliness and provided a microclimate that was more suitable for the human beings who lived in it. Even more important, they enabled the production of the agricultural resources that allowed the Persians to create and sustain their vast empire. D. R. Lightfoot, a professor of geography, asserted that 'a history of *qanat* irrigation provides a catalyst for understanding how successive waves of empire made the lands they occupied life-sustaining.'[10] The Parthian and Sasanid successors to the Achaemenids continued to develop the qanat network both in Persia itself and in the conquered lands. This Persian control over the water supply, in what was naturally a harsh environment, goes a long way towards explaining the endurance of Persia and the strength of its identity throughout the ages.

EIGHT

ALEXANDER OF MACEDON AND THE HELLENISTIC INTERLUDE

The world of the ancient Greeks was surrounded by non-Greek peoples who nevertheless over time came to be highly influenced by Greek civilization. Important among such peoples were the Macedonians, who lived on the northern fringes of the Greek world. They looked southwards to Greece and in time absorbed a great deal of what the great classical civilization had to offer. By the fourth century BC the sons of the Macedonian aristocracy, and especially of the royal house, were sent to Athens or other Greek cities to complete their education. Athenian philosophers would also be hired to be tutors in either Macedonia or in Greece itself.

The young king Alexander, who ascended the Macedonian throne in 336 BC following the assassination of his father Philip II, was steeped in all aspects of Greek culture. He considered Macedonia to be very much part of the Hellenic world and as such his principal objective as king was to maintain the security and well-being of this world. To the young Macedonian monarch this could be accomplished only by the fulfilment of two principal objectives: the unification of the Hellenic cities into a single powerful state, and the removal, forever, of the Persian danger. Although the age of warfare between the Greeks and the Persians had by that time come to an end, at least for the time being, the great eastern empire still appeared to be a menacing and dangerous neighbour on the other side of the Aegean. It was too close for comfort and, despite considerable contraction over the previous century, it still held a dominating position over most of – if no longer almost all – the ancient world. The Achaemenids were certainly weaker than they had been in the past and this made the possibility of confronting them appear more realistic.

Almost as soon as he became king, Alexander determined to bring the situation to a head and to attack the Persians. The most he could probably have expected was to weaken their empire to such an extent that it would no longer be able to retain the dominant position it had enjoyed during the previous two centuries. In 334 BC Alexander crossed the Hellespont at the head of a large army. He was confronted at Granicus in northern Anatolia by an equally powerful Persian army commanded by the Shahanshah Darius III himself. In this battle the Macedonians were triumphant. Their heavily armed cavalry had little problem dispersing the Persian light horse and there were heavy Persian losses, including many of their leaders. This defeat shook the Persians to the core and it revealed a weakness at the heart of the empire that may have been suspected but had not been fully accepted. In military terms, it opened up the whole of the west of Anatolia to the Macedonians.

The next confrontation with Darius was in 333 BC at Issus, close to the Gulf of Alexandretta on the southern edge of Anatolia. According to Greek observers of the battle a mere 35,000 Macedonians faced 'a vast horde' of Asiatics. While the Greek historians, especially Herodotus, almost always exaggerated the numbers of their opponents, and contrasted this with the relatively small numbers of Greeks, Alexander's army would certainly have been considerably smaller than at Granicus, as large numbers had been left to garrison the territory already occupied. Nevertheless, Alexander was once more victorious in this second battle, and the Persians were forced to retreat after again sustaining heavy losses.

It was after this battle that Alexander moved southwards around the shores of the Mediterranean and entered Egypt. This was no longer within the Persian Empire but the invasion by Alexander substantially increased the size of the Greek presence in the Mediterranean. On the northern coast of Egypt, on the edge of the Nile Delta, he founded the first of what were to be many new cities. This was Alexandria, and it was to prove to be one of his greatest legacies. From then on he came to see the new cities he founded as beacons of Hellenic civilization built in the midst of the barbarous Asiatic world.

In 331 BC Alexander moved back eastwards into northern Mesopotamia, where the third and final great battle with the Persians took place. This was on the plain of Gaugamela near the ancient Assyrian capital of Nineveh. The Persian army was without doubt far larger than that of the Macedonians, but the latter were more disciplined and organized, while the former included a considerable number of subject peoples, who proved difficult to control.[1] Once more Alexander was victorious and after that battle the Persian army disintegrated. The Greek phalanx, perfected by the Macedonians, played a major part in ensuring the defence of the Macedonian forces against the huge numbers mustered by the Persians.[2] Darius managed to escape eastwards but by this time he had few followers left; the last Achaemenid king was finally assassinated by Bessus, the satrap of Bactria. A little more than two centuries after Cyrus's great victory over the Medes at Pasargadae had inaugurated the rise of the Achaemenids, the empire came to an ignominious end in the bleak mountains of the east.

It has been said that the empire of the Medes did not actually come to an end but merely acquired new management. In some ways the same could be said of the Macedonian conquest. Following the death of Darius, Alexander was proclaimed Shahanshah. Clearly, the conqueror intended that the empire that had dominated the Middle East for so long should continue to exist, but now it would be the Macedonians, a people from the edge of Europe, who would be in charge. He then moved to complete his triumph by advancing on Persepolis, the ceremonial capital of the empire. After occupying the city, and when the great victory celebrations were over, he ordered it to be destroyed. It is not known why Alexander engaged in this act of wanton destruction. Some have suggested that he did it in an act of drunken madness; others propose that it was revenge for the Persian destruction during the invasions of Greece by Darius and Xerxes. Whatever the reason, it signified very clearly the end of the Achaemenid Empire and the beginning of Alexander's brief attempt to resurrect it as a Hellenistic one.

The Macedonians, and through them the Greeks, now dominated the ancient world. Yet Alexander's appetite for conquest was not satisfied. He still wanted to probe to the edges of that world and to discover what was there and what dangers to his new empire might still be lurking. His actions resembled those of Cyrus, and the ultimate result had many similarities with them. Leaving garrisons wherever he went, he took his army northwards into Central Asia. He occupied a large part of the basin of the Oxus and Jaxartes, that Central Asia in Mesopotamia into which the Achaemenids had long before penetrated a little too far, and where Cyrus the Great had met his end. From there he took his army southwards through the mountains of Bactria using the Khyber Pass to invade India. In this way he added most of the basin of the Indus to his conquests. From there he turned back westwards and returned by sea through the Persian Gulf to Mesopotamia. He eventually arrived in Babylon, where he had decided the capital of his new empire was to be built.

The empire that Alexander planned was to be modelled on that of the Persians. Although a sworn enemy of the Persians, the Greeks showed the greatest respect for their foe and this respect continued even after the calamitous Persian defeat. Herodotus summarized the education of a Persian boy: 'They train them from the age of five to the age of twenty to do three things, and three things only: to ride and to shoot and to speak the truth.'³ Arnold Toynbee considered that the most impressive of all Greek testimonies to Persian virtues was Alexander himself. As a demonstration of his intentions, Alexander married Roxane, the daughter of Oxyartes, a Sogdian chieftain, and encouraged his generals to marry into the conquered people.⁴ Despite encountering resistance from the Macedonians, he also began the enlistment of Persian soldiers into his army. In some ways Alexander can be regarded as being less the founder of a new empire than as the last of the Achaemenids. His aim was to bring about a kind of fusion of Greeks and Persians into a new and unified world order. His ideal was not so much to destroy the Persian Empire as to resurrect it as a Hellenistic one. The two 'greats' – Cyrus and Alexander – certainly had much in common. However, while Cyrus created the first world empire,

Alexander's ideal was not to become a reality. The king died in Babylon in 323 BC at the young age of 33.[5] The creation of the new Hellenistic empire was still on the drawing board and Alexander's great plans were to remain unfulfilled.

There is an interesting, if understandable, ambiguity in later sources on Alexander, or Iskander, as he is known in eastern sources. Western accounts generally portray him in heroic terms as a figure who triumphantly brought Hellenistic culture to the East. Indeed, in many sources he is transformed from a historic figure into a semi-mythical or legendary hero of romance, becoming an icon of heroic kingship and courtly idealism similar to King Arthur in the European tradition.

Persian sources are more ambiguous. Alexander is described in them as a great statesman and heroic leader, but he is also remembered as the destroyer of Persian cities such as Susa and, particularly, Persepolis. Ferdowsi in his *Shahnameh* describes how Alexander smashed the *taqdis*, the mythical throne of the Iranian kings, but nonetheless Ferdowsi attempts to give him some legitimacy as heir to the Persian throne by presenting him as the half-brother of Darius, the last Achaemenid king. Later, when writing of the Sasanid period, he reverts to describing Alexander as evil and destructive and an enemy of the Persian people.

The Zoroastrian tradition has no such ambiguity, presenting Alexander definitively as the killer of many Magi and as having extinguished the sacred flame and destroyed many fire temples. In later Zoroastrian writings, Alexander shares with Angra Mainyu the title of *Guzastag* – the Accursed.

Following their king's death, the Macedonians were left triumphant but leaderless. They were the rulers of a vast empire, but what they fundamentally lacked was an emperor able to take it forward. Most significantly, they failed to replicate the unity that had been created by the Persian Empire. It is said that when those around his deathbed asked Alexander who he wished to nominate as his successor, he replied 'the best'.[6] Who 'the best' may have been remains a mystery and, with no accepted successor, those who had been closest to Alexander – his generals – began to dispute the succession among themselves. These were the *Diadochi* – the

Successors – and eventually it was resolved that the only solution was for the empire to be divided among them.

It was Seleucus who became the ruler of that part of the empire centring on Mesopotamia and the historic Persian lands. The heart of his empire was Mesopotamia and in it he built his capital Seleucia, just to the north of Babylon. It thus largely accorded with the geo-political structure of the empire as envisaged by Alexander, who would have made Babylon his capital, but there was little sign of the fusion of Greeks and Persians he had envisaged as being funda-mental to his new world order. The great project of Hellenization remained and the Seleucid Empire was central to this Hellenistic period in Persian history. Alexander had intended this empire to be based on the establishment of Hellenic cities throughout the Persian Empire, as centres for the spread of Greek civilization, and during his short reign he began this process with considerable vigour. The city-state, the *polis*, was the basic unit of government in Greece itself and this was a model Alexander intended to extend throughout his empire. It was to have been an empire of city-states, thus achieving on a massive scale what the Macedonians had orig-inally desired to bring about in the Aegean world itself. The first and most famous of these city-states founded by Alexander had been Alexandria in Egypt, and this was soon followed by the estab-lishment of more Alexandrias as far north as Central Asia and as far east as India. They were seen as being the bedrock of the Hellenization of the world and as firm outposts of his new city-state empire.

While the legacy of Alexander was split up among the *Diadochi*, what did come into existence was a massive free-trade area cover-ing the whole of the Hellenistic world and extending from the Mediterranean to the Indus. Greek became the lingua franca and Greek merchants and administrators were placed in positions of power. Despite the political divisions, the Hellenization of the world was well under way.

The intention of the new Greek world order was that empire and *polis*, for so long set apart as confrontational opposites, would be fused into one. This remained an ideal, and the only place in which it was partly realized was the kingdom of Seleucus. The two principal elements of an alternative geopolitical world structure remained for the most part unfulfilled fundamentals.[7] It was Seleucia that came nearest to the fulfilment of the Hellenistic ideal, but it was not to remain so for long. In the end it would be imperialism that triumphed, and when it did so the *polis* would become not its partner but its victim.[8] Within a few centuries there would be many forgotten Alexandrias dotted throughout the lands of the old Persian Empire.[9]

The Seleucid dynasty retained its hold for little more than a century. Around 150 BC another group of nomadic people moved southwards from Central Asia. These were the Parthians, and they gradually displaced the Seleucids. They took over much of the east of what had been the Persian Empire and soon came into contact with Rome, the power that was moving into a dominant position in the Mediterranean and which was extending its sphere of influence eastwards. In 53 BC the Romans were roundly defeated by the warlike Parthians at Carrhae in Mesopotamia, and that called a halt for some time to their eastern ambitions.

In the second century AD, at the height of its power, Rome again moved eastwards into Mesopotamia, thus once more coming into conflict with the Parthians. By that time the latter had become a diminished force and presented far less of a threat than they had before. The Romans had little difficulty in occupying the region and added it to what by that time had become an enormous empire. However, Rome was soon to be confronted with a far more formidable and permanent opponent in the East, and this was brought about by the rise of a new Persian Empire, which threw off the Parthians. This new empire then sought to model itself on the Achaemenids and to emulate their achievements. After their fall centuries earlier, the Achaemenids had left a strong political and cultural legacy in the Mediterranean and the Middle East. This was now to be used by their successors to resurrect the ancient empire and to give it a role in the fast-changing Middle Eastern world.

NINE

EMPIRE REVIVED: THE SASANIDS

At its maximum extent the territory controlled by the Parthians included most of modern Iran, Mesopotamia, Eastern Anatolia and Afghanistan. They endeavoured to prove their right to rule by claiming to have links with the Achaemenid dynasty but, given their relatively recent Central Asian origins, none of these claims were at all convincing. As with earlier empires, Mesopotamia became the main centre of their power and their capital was Ctesiphon, a city they built on the Tigris adjacent to Seleucia, the Seleucid capital. The Parthian Empire lasted until the middle of the third century AD, but their grip on power was already weakening by the second century and by the third, much of their empire was in turmoil.

In AD 114, Mesopotamia was occupied by a Roman army under the command of the emperor Trajan. The Parthian capital was now in Roman hands and the Parthians were forced to retreat eastwards. However, Mesopotamia did not remain in the Roman Empire for very long and the Romans soon moved back west to a more defensible frontier in Syria. From then on Parthian rule became ever more tenuous.

At this time invaders from Eastern Europe and Central Asia had been the rulers of Persia since the fall of the Achaemenid Empire over 500 years earlier. In the early part of the third century, during the period of conflict between Rome and the Parthians, the Middle East was rapidly descending into chaos. It was at that time of troubles that an attempt was made to resurrect the Achaemenid Empire. The main insurrection against the Parthians was led by

Ardashir, a native of the province of Pars, the old Achaemenid heartland and the centre of their rule. Ardashir (Artaxerxes) gained control of Pars as early as 208 and, using Pars as his base, he conquered the territories adjacent to it. He finally defeated the Parthians in 224 in the battle of Hormozdgan, in which the last Parthian king was killed.

Two years later, in 226, Ardashir, who claimed to be able to trace his ancestry back to the Achaemenids, proclaimed himself Shah. In so doing he inaugurated the Sasanian dynasty, which ruled over what was in effect the second Persian Empire for the next four centuries. Ardashir moved his capital from Pars to the Parthian city of Ctesiphon, and in so doing gave his new empire a decidedly western orientation from the outset.

Having dealt successfully with a number of opponents, including the Kushans in the east and the Armenians in the west, the Sasanids soon found themselves in conflict with Rome, which was still the dominant imperial power in the west. The conflict of these two powers for dominance over the Middle East was to last for many centuries. For both, this conflict was central to their foreign policies and the geopolitical structures of both states were

Naqsh-i Rustam, showing the tombs of Darius alongside those of his predecessors.

soon organized with victory over the other as their principal objective.

Ardashir chose to leave his home province of Pars and to move his capital to Ctesiphon, well to the west of his Persian homeland. At the same time the Roman Empire had been engaged in a similar process in reverse, by relocating its centre of power in the east. The emperor Constantine, who ascended the imperial throne in 306, made the decision to relocate his capital from Rome and finally chose the site of the old Greek city of Byzantium on the Bosphorus, renaming it Constantinople. This city was at the meeting point of the Aegean and the Black Sea and consequently was strategically located as the headquarters from which campaigns in the east could be most effectively conducted. In later centuries it was to become the centre of Orthodox Christianity and the greatest city in Europe.[1] The move to the east was a recognition both that this was in most ways the richest and most important part of the empire and also that the greatest danger to the empire came from this direction. Both the Persian and the Roman capitals were therefore 'forward' capitals in the sense used by Vaughan Cornish.[2] This means that the two capitals were not only the centres of imperial power but bases for defence and, if successful, for further territorial expansion.

Early on in the period of Sasanid rule, the new dynasty organized their empire internally in much the same way as the Achaemenids had done. The satrapies (provinces) were brought back, each of them ruled by a satrap (governor) who was responsible to the Shahanshah himself. Most importantly, the old legal system, the 'laws of the Medes and the Persians', which had been such an important unifying feature of the Achaemenid Empire, was re-established.[3] The Zoroastrianism of the Achaemenids was revived and proclaimed the official state religion. As had been the case with the earlier dynasty, religion provided yet another convenient justification for the Sasanid rulers.

Shapur I and the Unknown Enemy, rock carving at Naqsh-i Rustam.

AD 226–41	Ardashir, founder of the Sasanid dynasty proclaimed Shahanshah
241–72	Shapur I: triumph of Persia over Rome; Manicheanism in the ascendant
273–6	Vahram II: strict Zoroastrianism and persecution of the Manicheans
276–93	Vahram II: persecutions continued
293–302	Narseh Persian defeat by the Roman emperor Diocletian
310–79	Shapur II: Zoroastrian persecutions continued and the conflict with Rome intensified
531–79	Khusrau I: golden age of the arts and sciences
591–628	Khusrau II: defeat by Byzantium
640–51	Yazdegerd III: defeat by the Arabs and end of the dynasty

The Sasanid dynasty's most important reigns.

Ardashir's successor, his son Shapur I, like his father took the title 'Shahanshah', but also added 'of Iran and non-Iran', thus clearly demonstrating his imperial ambitions. During his thirty-year reign he was involved more than anything else in wars on the frontiers. He faced a continuing threat from the Kushans in the east and, of course, from Rome in the west, and in dealing with these powers he adopted a kind of 'Schlieffen Plan' strategy.[4]

He first attacked the Kushans and, marching his army into their heartland in northern India, finally defeated them. As a result of this victory he secured an extended eastern frontier that stretched from the Oxus eastwards to the Indus, and incorporated the territories of modern Afghanistan and much of Uzbekistan into his realm.

Shapur then turned against Rome, which he saw rightly as being the greatest danger to his empire. Advancing westwards, he reached the Mediterranean and secured Antioch. In 259, in an impressive victory over the Romans at Edessa, the emperor Valerian was captured and brought back as a prisoner. The Roman prisoners were set to work to build bridges and roads, which further secured the western marches of the empire. This victory is commemorated in a rock relief at Naqsh-i Rustam in which the Roman emperor is on his knees and seen surrendering to the victorious Shapur.

The fact that the rocks in this area were used for such carvings was another link with the Achaemenids, who had used this workable stone for a variety of bas-reliefs and cuneiform inscriptions. The tombs of both Cyrus and Darius are, of course, located in this region, as are the sites of Pasargadae and Persepolis. The first of the Sasanid rock carvings depicts the investiture of Ardashir himself, and there is another of the king confronting a hostile Parthian nobleman. In this way Pars was confirmed as being the 'sacred space' of the Persians, in which their history was depicted in stone.[5]

While Shapur continued the internal organization programme of his predecessor, during his reign the position of the Zoroastrian religion was by no means secure. It was officially the state religion, but since the time of the Achaemenids considerable changes had been taking place within it. These produced a variant of Zoroastrianism known as Zurvanism, which flourished during the Sasanid period. Zurvanism aims to address the problem of how Ahuramazda could produce evil. This problem was dealt with by introducing Zurvan, 'Time', which is the origin of all things and is morally neutral. The religion then is based on the struggle of the twin offspring of Zurvan, Ohrmazd (Good) and Ahriman (Evil). Unlike Ahuramazda, Ohrmazd is not a creator god but embodies and represents good in the world. While Zurvanism thus introduced a new metaphysical interpretation of the world, it did not alter the idea of the dynasty having its own special relationship with Ohrmazd, as it had done with Ahuramazda. As with the Zoroastrianism of the Achaemenids, the priests of the religion were the Magi and its places of worship were the fire temples. The Magi had a quasi-official status and their activities were closely bound up with those of the dynasty itself. It was through them that the actions of the dynasty were approved by the god. Some complex dogmas were introduced into Zurvanism, linking history and myth in supplying explanations of the cosmos. These included the existence of a number of different ages, each with their own particular characteristics. In the final age a saviour appears who ushers in a kind of golden era for mankind. An

Shapur I is victorius over the Roman emperor Valerian, rock carving near the tomb of Darius I at Naqsh-i Rustam.

element of polytheism also crept into the religion and both the sun god Mithra and the star god Sirius were celebrated in festivals and were themselves objects of worship.[6]

Despite Zurvanism having been proclaimed as the state religion by his predecessor, Shapur himself looked elsewhere. He took a considerable interest in the teachings of the prophet Mani and during his reign the religion of Manichaenism made a considerable impact in the Sasanid Empire.[7] While this new 'universal' religion owed much to Zoroastrianism, it also drew on Christianity and Buddhism. It has been speculated that Shapur's promotion of the new religion was in part a reaction against the growing power of the Magi, the

Zoroastrian priestly class, and his fear that their power could challenge his own. However, Shapur's enthusiasm for the new religion was not shared by his successors, and under the next king, Bahram I, its followers were persecuted and the prophet Mani was himself arrested, tortured and put to death.

Shapur's victory over Valerian, while seen by the Persians as evidence of their superiority over Rome, did not really produce anything conclusive in relations with Rome, and the eastern frontier also soon became unsettled once more. However, under Shapur II, whose seventy-year reign stretched throughout the greater part of the fourth century, the Persians were again successful both in the east and the west. Following the conversion of the Roman emperor Constantine to Christianity, the religious question came to loom large in relations between the two empires. Successive Sasanid sovereigns pursued very different policies towards the Christians living in their territories and this often depended on the state of relations with Rome at that particular time. Another religious problem for Persia was that of the Mazdakites, an egalitarian religious sect deriving from Manicheanism. This, together with numerous other factors, internal and external, contributed to a gradual weakening of the hold of the Sasanids.

The Sasanids had one last period of success during the reign of Khusrau I, in the sixth century. Khusrau's reign proved to be a period in which the relations of the various factions in the country were fairly stable. There were reforms of the taxation system and the organization of the army, and the fortifications along the frontiers were strengthened. The Nestorians, the Christian community in Persia, were granted freedom of worship and a 'perpetual peace' was signed with the Byzantines (though, as with previous such treaties, this did not in fact last very long).

It was during this period that Rome and Persia were brought together by external threats, notably the Huns, who invaded both empires in the fifth century. The Romans and the Persians joined forces to oppose these barbarians from Central Asia. In addition to this, during the reign of Khusrau II, the Sasanid king was forced to seek aid from the Byzantines when faced with an attempted *coup d'état* by the army. The aid was given and the coup failed, but the Byzantines extracted a heavy price for their help and extended their frontiers well to the east. However, this situation proved to be unstable and did not last long. Unwilling to accept the humiliation, a few years later Khusrau attacked the Byzantine Empire and succeeded in making spectacular territorial gains. Syria, Armenia, Palestine and Eastern Anatolia were all occupied. The Persians made further inroads to the west into the heart of the Byzantine Empire, even at one time besieging Constantinople itself. The Persians then moved southwest into Egypt, bringing that country back under their rule after many centuries. As a result of this massive reversal of fortunes, by the end of the reign of Khusrau the empire was larger than it had been at any time since the Achaemenids.

However, this triumph was of fairly brief duration. In 610 a new Byzantine emperor, Heraclius, ascended the throne. He was young, vigorous and a gifted strategist. He immediately ordered more offensive tactics against the Persians and was soon able to turn the tables on them. By this time the Persians had been greatly weakened by the earlier efforts they had been forced to make, and Shah Khusrau II had become deeply unpopular as conditions in his kingdom deteriorated. As their armies were pushed back by the forces of Heraclius, in 628 a coup took place in which the unpopular shah was murdered. The result of this was not an improvement but the beginning of a descent into chaos in the empire. Over the next ten years, while Byzantium strengthened its frontiers and consolidated its gains, Persia gradually disintegrated into a land of battling warlords. It was during this time that a massive change took place in the Middle East that was to have profound implications for the whole region and indeed for the world.

In Arabia to the south in 622, the year in which the forces of Heraclius defeated the Persians at Issus, other, equally momentous events were taking place. As a result of these the centuries-old Roman–Persian conflict would soon be relegated to history. In that year a former Arab merchant named Muhammad, who had for some time been preaching a form of monotheism which was gradually evolving into a new religion, fled Mecca and established himself in Medina. This flight is known as the Hegira, a seminal

The investiture of Ardashir, rock carving at Naqsh-i Rustam.

event in the establishment of what was to become the new religion of Islam. Six years later, while the Persian king Khusrau was assassinated and the country descended into chaos, Muhammad, by then widely recognized in Arabia as a prophet, was able to return to Mecca and embark on the writing of the Koran, the holy book of the new religion. The Prophet Muhammad died in 632 and his followers were left with the problem of what exactly they were to do to disseminate his message. The decision was taken to establish what was in effect to become a theocratic empire, the head of which was to be known as the caliph, the successor to the Prophet. The first of these caliphs was Abu Bakr, the father-in-law of Muhammad, who embarked on a policy of 'holy war' in order to bring the lands adjacent to Arabia into the Islamic fold. For this purpose he began the creation of a powerful and highly motivated army that was soon to change the whole face of the Middle East and the lands around the Mediterranean.

The first attack by the caliphate was against the two ancient empires of Persia and Byzantium, which had together dominated the Middle East for centuries. They sustained the full force of the initial Arab invasion, the aim of which was to bring them both into the fold of the new religion. As a result of their recent defeat by the Byzantines, the Persians were the weaker of the two and the less able to put up any real resistance. In 637 Ctesiphon, the Sasanid capital, was captured and from there the Arabs moved steadily northwards into the Persian heartland. In 642, at Nihawand, the Persian army was finally defeated and the last Shahanshah, Yazdegerd, the grandson of Khusrau II, fled northwards into Central Asia. His assassination at Merv in 651 brought an end to the dynasty and also to that ancient Persian Empire which had been revived by the Sasanids. The Persian Empire was now incorporated into the caliphate and came under the direct rule of the Arabs from their far-off capital at Medina. In contrast to this, and despite repeated attacks, the Byzantines were strong enough to hold back the Arab armies and this, for a time, prevented any further Islamic movement directly westwards into Europe.

This failure contrasted with the rapid success achieved by the Arabs against the Persians, and contributed to the Arab decision to make their next thrust eastwards into Asia rather than westwards into Europe. Considerable military resources were put into the eastward move into Central Asia, a move that was eventually to bring Islam to the Indian subcontinent. The subjection of the Persians to the Arabs was in many ways comparable to the arrival of yet another new dynasty in former times. However, while these earlier dynasties had attempted to link themselves to the Achaemenids, the arrival of the Arabs was different and produced a massive cultural transformation in the country. This was the result of the religion the Arabs brought with them, which was the principal justification for their conquests. The coming of Islam entailed the erection of entirely new religious buildings – mosques – which now replaced the fire temples. These, together with the Arab secular buildings, eventually produced a completely new man-made landscape in the country. Islamic sharia law was introduced and Arabic became both the language of religion and the official language of government. However, despite this massive transformation, much of what had been most characteristically Persian did in fact survive, and this became the basis of that legacy which Persia was to pass on to the Asiatic and subsequently the European world.

ISLAMIC PERSIA AND PERSIAN ISLAM

The Arab conquest of Persia took place with astonishing speed. One of the two great historic empires that had dominated the Middle East for many centuries collapsed within a decade of the invasion by what were, by comparison with Persia at the time, a relatively primitive desert people. Muslim chroniclers themselves referred to the conquest as a miracle. Undoubtedly one of the most important causes of this sudden collapse was the weakness of the country following its final and unsuccessful war with Byzantium, which had only just come to an end. Thus by defeating one of the two great Middle Eastern empires, the victor had paved the way for the complete transformation of the region. There was also another cause, and this was the favourable reception that Islam received in so many of the countries that the Arabs invaded. Its simple monotheism, the removal of ruling classes – which had often been oppressive and disliked – and the preaching of egalitarianism were for large sections of the population very positive features of the new religion. The remission of taxes for conversion to Islam was another bonus, making the arrival of the Arabs more of a liberation than an occupation. What was now being offered seemed to be a distinct improvement on what had been there before.

For the great majority of the Persian population this was certainly the case. Their Sasanid rulers had become remote and were embroiled in endless wars. The heavy burden of taxation, which the people had been called upon to bear during the final war with Byzantium, had made the dynasty highly unpopular during the final years of its rule. The reality was that who their rulers were was of little consequence to the people, so long as they were not unbearably oppressive and were able to maintain law and order. Peace was something that the population desired more than anything after such a long period of war. The remission of taxes was certainly an easy and non-violent way of ensuring acceptance of the new rulers, and mass conversion to Islam took place with considerable ease.

For the former Sasanid ruling class, the situation was very different. They had been overthrown by the Arabs and so had lost their privileged position in society. In most cases the estates of the landowners, the *dihqan*, were confiscated and became the property of the caliph. In other cases they were taken over by local Arab chieftains, who in this way became the inheritors of the wealth and property of their predecessors.[1]

It was not at all easy for the Arabs to do away entirely with the ancient civilization of Persia and to replace it with their own. The indigenous civilization was far too strong and ingrained for this to happen and in many ways the opposite began to take place. Almost immediately, Persian civilization influenced the conquerors and this soon brought about many changes in Islam itself. Alessandro Bausani even maintained that: 'It is quite unreal to equate the Arabs with Islam and the Persians with non-Islam. The Persian conquest marked a vital stage in the development of Islam as we know it today.'[2] The success of Islam in Persia was by no means entirely an Arab achievement. The Arabs may have been the conquerors, but there were many native Persians who took rapidly to the new religion and put their particular stamp upon it. This was most especially the case in Pars, where the link with Islam appears to have been particularly strong from the early years (see Chapter Fourteen). Over the following two centuries, Persia gradually developed its own particular brand of Islam, which became important in determining the evolution of the whole Islamic world, as well as of Persia itself.

With the arrival of the Arabs, the language of the conquerors became the official language of the country, as it did in all other parts of their empire. The Arabic script was introduced and, as with the language, this had to be learned by the old governing class if they were to have any role in the new Islamic province of the caliphate. The Koran, the holy text of Islam, was of course written in Arabic, and in order to begin to understand the new religion a knowledge of that language was essential. While Zoroastrianism and even some of the cults survived and even flourished in the more remote parts of the country, many of its temples were taken over by the new rulers and converted into mosques. This was usually a temporary measure and soon mosques were being built, many of which were later considered to be among the most beautiful anywhere in the Islamic world. *Madrasas* – religious schools – also soon appeared and a new class of Persians educated in the Arabic language began to emerge. It was from this educated class that the new Islamic priesthood came into being. However, although the Persian educated classes learned Arabic, the language of the country remained Persian, and although the Arabic script soon replaced the Persian script, the language itself continued to be used. Arabic always remained a foreign tongue, although knowledge of it was essential to secure advancement in the new world of which Persia was now a part. However, it was quite evident that Persia was very different from the rest of the Islamic Middle East and from the beginning there were many revolts against Arab rule there.

The whole question of the succession had been a contentious one since the death of the Prophet in 632, and at first it had been in the hands of his blood relatives and his closest companions. This period of the so-called 'orthodox caliphs' came to an end with the assassination of Ali, Muhammad's son-in-law, in 661. After much discussion, the Umayyads, who claimed a distant kinship with the Prophet, secured the caliphate. This Umayyad caliphate lasted for a little over a century, and during this period there was considerable dissatisfaction in Persia, and elsewhere in the Arab world, with what was very quickly seen as a remote and autocratic rule. The autocratic Sasanids had been replaced by an Islamic dynasty that was behaving in all too similar a manner. In 750 came a series of rebellions throughout Islam, the one in Persia being led by Abu Muslim. The Umayyads were toppled and the caliphate was taken over by Abu al-Abbas of the Hashemite tribe. It was he who established the Abbasid caliphate, which ruled the empire for the next 500 years.

Initially, the Abbasids made many promises to the dissatisfied people, and at first this made the prospect of their rule attractive to the Persians. One of these was that the capital of the caliphate would be moved to a more central location. In the event, the Abbasids moved the capital from Damascus in Syria to Baghdad in Mesopotamia, an outcome that was seen as very satisfactory by the Persian rebels. This new capital was within the territory of the old Sasanid Empire and was very close to the legendary city of Babylon and, more importantly, to Ctesiphon, the Sasanid capital. Located as it was within the land that had been part of earlier Persian empires, and in the historic 'capital region' of the Middle East, this opened up the prospect of strengthening the Persian influence in the Islamic world. The new city of Baghdad soon developed into a great centre of learning and much of this was the work of Persian-speaking scholars.[3] The following centuries were a time of great advance in science and the arts in the Islamic world and the Persian contribution, as previously discussed, proved to be considerable.

Nevertheless, there was still great dissatisfaction in Persia and the clash between the Arab and Persian cultures remained very much in evidence. The fact that the country, which had been for so long the great empire of the Middle East and in many ways its centre, was now reduced to being a part of another empire was something that was difficult for the Persians to accept. It was this that underlay the frequent rebellions and the rise of local dynasties, many of which were successful in taking control of large parts of the country. Important among these dynasties were the Tahirids, who were made governors of Khorasan by the caliph but who rebelled against him and established their own quasi-independent state. Later there were the Saffarids from Sijistan who spread out into Khorasan in the later ninth century. Most important and successful was the Samanid dynasty, the founder of which, Saman-khudat, claimed descent from the Sasanids. The original heart of Samanid power had been Transoxiana, well away from the principal centres of Arab rule. From there the Samanids moved southwards into Khorasan and Sijistan, and then eastwards into Afghanistan. The caliph Al-Mamun had considerable respect for the Persians and granted the Samanids governorship of a number of provinces, including Samarkand, Ferghana and Herat.

It was in this way that the dynasty built up its strength, eventually becoming virtually independent of the caliph. While Transoxiana remained of considerable importance to them, they established their capital in Khorasan at Nishapur, a city from which they were able to exercise effective control over most of the east of the country. This dynasty provided a link with the pre-Islamic past and also, through the Sasanids, even back to the Achaemenids. In this way, although great changes had taken place since the Islamic conquest, there remained a certain sense of continuity back to the remote past of the country. This gave the new dynasties an element of the legitimacy that they all sought in order to justify their rule. It was this sense of past greatness that inspired the Persians to think of themselves as different from, and in so many ways superior to, the caliphate.

As a result, the ancient heritage re-emerged alongside Islam, which for the previous two centuries had made vigorous attempts to suppress it in favour of its own. By the tenth century the caliphs in Baghdad were in no position to bring the rebellious subjects to heel and were forced even to endorse the new situation by giving impressive titles to the new rulers. It was from this time on that the Persians began again to take great pride in their own identity, and it was out of this that the *Shuubiyya* movement developed, which has been seen by some as an early form of nationalism. It looked back to the ancient empire and its achievements and did much to emphasize that Persian sense of superiority over the Arabs. While the Persians saw themselves as having been a great and historic civilization, the Arabs increasingly came to be looked down upon as desert nomads having little real culture. The Persians came to resent being subjected to control by a people to whom they felt superior and for whom in many ways they felt contempt. The *Shuubiyya* movement strengthened their desire to separate themselves from the Arab caliphate and to revert to their historic independence.[4]

With Arabic control – and even that of Islam itself – loosening, not only was a return to independent statehood possible, but so was a new flourishing of the Persian language and culture. This took place within what were strictly the Persian lands, as well as more widely throughout the extensive territory of the old Persian Empire. This renaissance was nowhere more visible than in Baghdad itself. At that time the Abbasid capital became one of the greatest centres of learning in the world and the Persian influence in this was very much in evidence.

By the time of the Samanid dynasty, which ruled for almost the whole tenth century, Persia had developed its own particular character, which was to make it from then on quite distinct from most of the rest of the Islamic world. This character was the result partly of developments that took place in Islamic times and partly of other characteristics derived from the earlier inheritance. By this time Islam itself was by no means monolithic and there was considerable religious diversity within it. In Persia such diversity was to a large extent the result of the survival of the Zoroastrian religion and the proliferation of sects that, in many ways, were related to this. The first Samanid leader Saman-khudat was himself a Zoroastrian, but he seems to have converted to Islam mainly because he felt it to be in his best interests to do so. He was by no means the first or the last to think in such terms. Many of the sects that emerged were syncretic, drawing on other religions, including Christianity and Buddhism. The Mazdakites were Zoroastrian extremists who were violently opposed to Islam. Manichaeism, which dated from the time of the Sasanid king Shapur I, was based on the teachings of the prophet Mani, who came from a Christian family. This also survived in places well into Islamic times. Another religious sect was Khorramdin, 'the happy religion', which represented an attempt to fuse Zoroastrianism and Islam.

While the Samanids, and the dynasties that had preceded them, were centred in Khorasan and the east of the country, the west behaved quite differently. In the Zagros mountains and around the southern shores of the Caspian Sea there had always remained a strong feeling of independence. Here the Ziyarid dynasty gained power by the ninth century and soon subscribed to a very different version of Islam. Similarly, in the historic Persian homeland of Pars the sense of Persian identity remained very strong and here the Buyid dynasty gained power, with a similar sense of its own particular role.

In the context of Islam as a whole, these diverse ideas came to be centred on Shi'ism, which was a particularly Persian version of the religion. This had originated due to the problem of the caliph, the successor to the Prophet. The Shi'ites believed that the successor should be in the bloodline of the Prophet, in other words a member of the 'dynasty' of the Prophet, rather than quite different dynasties to which the Umayyads, and later the Abbasids, belonged. The Shi'ites therefore held the belief that the succession should be through the line of Ali, the son-in-law of the Prophet, who had also been the last of the orthodox caliphs. It was believed that Ali had inherited the Prophet's *wilayah*, his spiritual qualities, and had passed these on to his own sons, Hasan and Husayn. Ali was assassinated by the Umayyads in 661 and his son Husayn, grandson of the Prophet and claimant to the caliphate, was assassinated in 680 at Karbala near Baghdad. Karbala then became for the Shi'a one of their holiest shrines, and the martyrdom of Husayn was from then on commemorated there in the lunar month of Muharram. This led to the Shi'ite belief in the Twelve Imams, beginning with Ali and continuing through his successors. The line of succession continued until 878, when the last of the Twelve, al-Muntazar, withdrew from the world to return only when a new age was born. In addition to this, there was a further dimension to Shi'ism that linked it to ancient Persia. A legend appeared that Husayn had been married to one of the daughters of Yazdegerd III, the last of the Sasanid kings. In this way a sense of continuity could be established between Islam and the pre-Islamic past. Out of this Islam then came to be seen as not just something imposed and alien but as the heir to the earlier state and its rulers. The legitimacy of the new rulers of Persia was based not just on religious belief but on this other firm belief that the blood of the Sasanids flowed in the veins of the true successors to the Prophet.

In the early eleventh century new conquerors arrived on the scene. These were the Seljuk Turks who, like so many before them, came from Central Asia. There they had converted to Islam but they were unwelcome to the Persians not only because they were yet another set of conquerors from the north but because they had espoused the Sunni version of Islam, which accepted the Abbasid caliphate and its primacy throughout the Islamic Empire. In 1055 came the conquest of Baghdad itself by the Seljuks, and the caliph, unable to resist this new and powerful intruder, granted their leader the title of 'sultan', meaning sovereign, which from then on became the title given to Seljuk and later to Ottoman rulers. While they established themselves as rulers of Persia by the use of force, they were from the outset regarded as aliens and the period of their rule was peppered by constant outbreaks of rebellion, mainly linked to Shi'a beliefs that were hostile to the Turks and their orthodox Sunni version of Islam. Other rebellions were motivated by extreme religious convictions, but many of them were also forms of proto-nationalism – one of the principal objectives of which was to re-establish the independence of the country.

It was this fusion of Shi'a beliefs and hostility to the conquerors that produced one of the early forms of proto-nationalism. This was the Ismaili sect, which originated in Syria but which spread from there to other parts of the Islamic world and eventually established itself strongly in northern Persia. While following the basic Shi'a doctrine, they believed that the Seventh Imam was actually Ismail – not Musa, his brother, who was believed by the orthodox Shi'a to have been the true imam. As a result of this, Ismail became the centre of veneration for this sect. Among these Ismailis were the more extreme Nizaris, who engaged in murder and built strongholds in the mountains from which they waged constant war on all who held opposing beliefs. They were led at the time by Hasan-i Sabbah and were known by the Crusaders as the Assassins. It came to be widely believed that they gained this name through their use of hashish in their rituals.[5]

The principal stronghold of the Assassins was the fortress of Alamut – the Eagle's Nest – established in 1090 in the Alborz mountains. They went on to build a chain of other strong and inaccessible fortresses throughout the area. Hasan-i Sabbah came to be known as Shaykh al-jabal, 'the master of the mountain', translated by the Crusaders as 'the old man of the mountain'. They gained a bad reputation, both among the Seljuks and the Crusaders, and were considered to be little more than the terrorists of the age. However, the truth seems to have been rather different, since the evidence shows the Nizaris to have engaged in a great deal of philosophical thought about religion. The Ismailis as a whole were widespread throughout Persia at this time and their religious ideas led to much thought about the nature of Islam and the development of its role in the world. They attempted to reconcile Hellenistic Gnosticism with Islam and had a profound effect on the future development of Islamic thinking.

By the thirteenth century, the Seljuk Turks, like so many conquerors before them, were much weakened and were quite unable to defend themselves from one of the most powerful and ruthless invaders ever to emerge from Central Asia. These were the Mongols under Genghis Khan and his successors, and by the middle of the thirteenth century they had not only defeated the Seljuks but had destroyed both the Assassins and the caliphate and had become the dominant force in the Middle East. However, the Mongol Empire soon split up into a number of constituent parts owing only a nominal allegiance to the Great Khan. The Il-Khan dynasty, which became the dominant power in the Middle East, lasted barely a century, and with the collapse of the caliphate the last semblance of unity in Islam came to an end. Persia also once more became lawless and for a time a variety of dynasties and sects held sway in different parts of the country.

This situation lasted until the end of the fifteenth century, when a new and strong ruler was at last able to reunite the country. This was Ismail, the first of the Safavid dynasty, which took power in 1500. The Safavids were Turkish-speakers who came from the Kurdish lands in the northwest of the country. Ismail, having defeated other contenders for power, was proclaimed *Shahanshah-i-Iran* in 1501. Most importantly, the Safavids were Shi'ites and were members of the Qizilbash – Red Head – order. Shah Ismail claimed descent from the seventh of the Twelve Imams and this put him firmly in the line of succession from the caliph Ali. While there seems to have been very little substance to this claim, it served to place the new dynasty in the bloodline of the Prophet and thus secured the legitimacy of its shahs as rulers of Iran. The Shi'a version of Islam was proclaimed to be the official religion of the country and conversion was made obligatory, with refusal to convert resulting in execution. The only exceptions to this were the Christians, who became a protected minority. During the reign of Ismail the lands conquered by this northern dynasty steadily increased, and, most significantly, the Persian homeland of Pars and Mesopotamia, political and economic heart of the Sasanid Empire, were added. For the first time since the Islamic conquest over 700 years earlier, Persia had become a powerful independent state and one that was very different from its Middle Eastern neighbours. Besides Persia itself, only in southern Mesopotamia was there another large population of Shi'a Muslims. Mesopotamia was particularly important to the Shi'a because of its historic sites, which were of especial significance to their religion. Most significant among them was Karbala, the place where Husayn, the son of Ali, had been murdered by the supporters of the Umayyads.

The most significant reign of the Safavid dynasty was that of Shah Abbas, known as 'The Great' (r. 1587–1628). He consolidated the dynasty's grip on supreme power and diminished the role of the Qizilbash, which had developed into a kind of powerful and self-perpetuating aristocracy. He established his own royal army, which was quite independent of them and very much under his direct control. This new army was made up largely of non-Persians, among them many Georgians and Armenians, and it was modelled on the Turkish Janissaries. This ensured that it was outside the Persian religious and political disputes that had made the country so turbulent for much of the time since the coming of Islam. Abbas also strengthened governmental control over the administration of the country and moved the capital to Isfahan, which was very centrally located. There he proceeded to build a most magnificent city, with mosques and palaces of great beauty in that Persian Islamic architectural style, which is considered to have produced some of the most splendid buildings in the Islamic world.

The reign of Shah Abbas was in many ways the culmination of this particular period in Persian history. The Safavids reigned from the beginning of the sixteenth century, a time considered by European historians to have been the beginning of modern history, until the eighteenth century, when many European political ideas had become fully developed and were being spread across the world through colonization. While such historical divisions and subdivisions cannot easily be applied to the Middle East, during this dynasty one can discern distinct threads of continuity linking the empire of ancient times to the modern era. In this way many aspects of the legacy of the ancient empire came to be present in the modern development of the country.

An important feature of this continuity was the search for legitimacy by claims of a common ancestry, not only with the Prophet Muhammad through Shi'ite Islam, but with the Shahanshahs, the Great Kings, themselves. Since the end of the Achaemenid Empire the successive rulers of Persia had sought to legitimize their rule by referring back to earlier rulers and dynasties. This search for continuity over the centuries, perhaps more than anything else, enabled the Persians to maintain their own particular sense of identity in a way in which the other peoples conquered by the Arabs never could. The feeling of being heirs to a great empire was retained and this led to the retention and encouragement of many other features, setting Persia well apart from its neighbours.

Important among these was the language, which from the Islamic conquest remained the means of communication of the bulk of the population. While the new conquerors introduced Arabic as the language of government and religion, it was taken up by only a small – though very important – minority. The first administrators of the new regime were themselves Arabs and the first teachers of the new religion were too. However, as Persians took on these roles, they were obliged to achieve a fluency in Arabic. Arabic also gained considerable importance as the language of commerce, and Arab traders, moving widely throughout Asia, brought their language with them. However, when the grip of the Arabs began to loosen in the time of the Samanids, Persian once more moved into a position of importance in most walks of life. By the time of the Safavids, Turkish had also become widespread. It had been brought by the Seljuks and had retained its importance after their fall. Turkish had been the original language of the Safavids, although they soon changed over to Persian. This then became the language that was of special importance in creating and maintaining the Persian sense of identity, and it was soon being used widely again. It was only in Islamic teaching that Arabic retained its special role. The Koran was in Arabic and remained so – the study of the holy book in the mosques necessitated the attainment of a good knowledge of that language.

Thus while Persia underwent immense changes throughout the Islamic period, the memory of the ancient civilization was never lost. While this is evident from the desire of successive rulers to seek legitimacy by proving their relationship to the former dynasties, there was also the history and legend present in the literary tradition. Central to this were the epic poems containing stories of early Persia. The most important of these was the *Shahnameh*, the 'Book of Kings' by Ferdowsi, which is largely the story of the early kings and heroes of Persia, discussed in Chapter Fifteen.

The Persia that emerged in the sixteenth century as a quite distinct and independent entity within the Islamic world was not in any sense an empire. In many ways it was beginning to develop along lines that were more similar to what was happening in Europe. There, with the break-up of Christendom and the formation of nation-states such as England and France, a post-imperial situation was evolving. The surviving elements of the ancient Persian Empire were being used to create a different, and more modern, political entity that during the following centuries remained more typical of geopolitical structures in Europe than in the Middle East. However, in the twentieth century the memory of the glorious past was to prove stronger than the desire to become a modern nation, and this was to produce one last attempt to resurrect the ancient empire. The importance of Persia in Asia had always remained considerable and it retained a strong influence on the way in which large parts of the continent evolved into modern times.

ELEVEN

FROM PERSEPOLIS TO SAMARKAND: THE PERSIAN LEGACY IN CENTRAL ASIA

The territory of Persia and its successive empires centred on the Middle East, a region which is, of course, contiguous with other parts of Asia. As a consequence of its proximity to both Central and South Asia, historically Persia has influenced, and been influenced by, the peoples of these regions. In the millennium following the fall of the Achaemenid Empire and its Hellenistic successor states, there were numerous invasions from Central Asia by Parthians, Turks and Mongols, all of whom conquered large parts of the Middle East and established powerful empires there. All of them incorporated the lands that had been part of the Achaemenid and Sasanid empires and their centres of power were also inherited from those earlier rulers. These incomers were inevitably influenced by the indigenous civilization of the lands they conquered.

In addition to this, over time Persia came to exercise considerable influence over adjacent Central Asia, and this was nowhere more in evidence than in the lands between the Caspian and the Aral seas. This influence was of crucial importance in changing this region from one dominated by nomadic pastoralists – 'barbarians' in Greek terms – to one of the few great civilizations to develop in the heart of Asia itself. From the very beginning, in the time of the Achaemenids, the Persians had sought to bring Central Asia into their sphere. It was from there that the Persians and their mentors the Medes had first come, and they were followed by many other migrants seeking the better life which they believed was to be found in the lands to the south. As a result, the Central Asian lands were always considered a danger and from the outset of their imperial venture the Persians sought to prevent more unwelcome immigrants from descending on their empire and disrupting their rule.[1] Persistent Persian interventions meant that over the centuries the adjacent parts of Central Asia became gradually more integrated politically, economically and culturally with Persia itself.

During the reign of Darius the Great, the Achaemenid Empire extended its control deep into Central Asia and at that time the whole of Transoxiana was brought under the rule of the Great King. During that reign the region was divided into satrapies for administrative purposes and a Persian governing class was established there. Similarly, under the Sasanids, and later the Arabs, there was further penetration into the region. With the Arab invasions, Islam also took hold and this was to prove of great significance in the transformation of the Islamic world in later centuries.

Economically, Transoxiana in particular was a most welcome addition to any empire. The great trading cities of Samarkand, Bukhara and Balkh were of considerable commercial importance, adding a great deal to the economic power of the state within which they were located. One of the main reasons for this was that they lay on the Silk Road, that great trading route stretching across Asia from Europe to China. While the two main termini of this routeway were Byzantium in the west and Xi'an, the capital of China, in the east, Samarkand, Bukhara, Tashkent and Merv all achieved great importance. They were the places where the traders from the west met and exchanged goods with those from the east. The trading domes of Bukhara are witness to the huge economic importance of that particular city. While silk was, of course, of considerable value in the trade, there were a great many other products, including tea, spices, precious stones, ceramics, metals and metal ornaments. This trade benefited the economies of the lands it passed through and, consequently, Asiatic rulers wished to ensure that the favoured route passed through their territory.[2] The most important routeway westwards from Samarkand and Bukhara passed through northern Persia to Tabriz and on to Byzantium, which was the major commercial city in medieval Europe. During the sixteenth century Shah Abbas, realizing the value of the route, attempted to divert it southwards through his new capital of Isfahan. While this had some success in view of the importance of the Safavid capital, the northern route still remained the preferred way for traders making for Byzantium.

Finally, Persian cultural influences in this area also go back to ancient times. Political and military penetration of the area brought with it the Persian language. Being the language of the rulers, it inevitably soon came to be used by those over whom they ruled. Before long the leading families of the region were learning to speak Persian and as a consequence the region's importance in the Persian world increased. The Samanids, the most successful of the independent dynasties that sought to break Persia away from the Arab caliphate, came originally from Balkh on the Oxus river south of Samarkand. They were Persian-speakers and had converted to Islam before moving south into Khorasan and Parsa. They not only extended their rule south, but penetrated northwards deeper into Central Asia, establishing a capital at Bukhara. In this way there was an overall displacement of Persian civilization northwards away from the *qalb* (heartland) of the caliphate and into an area where the establishment of an independent state proved far easier.

When the rule of the Samanids was replaced by that of the Turks, the same set of conditions prevailed. Like the Samanids, the Turks, the first of them being the Ghaznavids from Afghanistan, followed by the Seljuks from Central Asia, had also converted to Islam.[3] They conquered a land with an established language and cultural attainments and themselves soon became influenced by these. The symbiosis that this all produced must have been, in part at least, responsible for the fact that the whole period from the Samanid rule in the tenth century to the Turks in the eleventh was one in which science, learning and the arts flourished, and Persian Central Asia played an important part in this.

The reason for the significance of Central Asia in the dissemination of Persian Islamic culture is very similar to that for the cultural dissemination into other peripheral regions of the Islamic world, notably Moorish Spain. The hold of the caliphate was lesser in such remote regions and there was greater freedom for individual expression. The *qalb* of the Abbasid caliphate was Mesopotamia and its political centre was Baghdad. Besides being the capital and residence of the caliph, it also soon attained a wider religious and cultural role. By the ninth century, this Arab city had become the major centre of learning in all Islam, and scholars and scientists from other parts of the empire were attracted to its madrasas, libraries and institutions of learning. It became a melting pot for new ideas in physics, astronomy, geography and other sciences. However, by the tenth century a religious and scholarly elite had become entrenched there and was increasingly reluctant to accept any new ideas that might conflict with their own. Said and Khan, in their biography of Al-Biruni, the Persian scholar born in AD 973, observed the wider implications of this development:

> As long as the work of translations and assimilations of foreign knowledge was going on, the centralization of scientific and literary activities at Baghdad proved beneficial. Under the vigilance of the caliphs, the work became organized and systematic and its accomplishment was guaranteed by the immense resources of the caliphate. But after this phase was completed, the centralization of the literary life became an impediment to further progress. A scholar who wanted to gain recognition had to go to Baghdad, where the already entrenched *ulema* and scholars made the entry of any new rival very difficult. The point is well illustrated by the episode of Ziryab, a Persian scholar from Transoxiana who was forced to leave Baghdad due to the envy of his teachers.[4]

Accompanying the hardening of attitudes in Baghdad came the weakening of the Abbasid caliphate and the loosening of its grip on Islam. This was another factor in making Baghdad less attractive, and it encouraged the dispersal and decentralization of learning and knowledge. This produced greater diversity in the Islamic world than was possible when one leading city dominated most fields of activity.

Central Asia was one of the most important centres in this new era, and many of the leading scholars and scientists of the age came from there. Many of its cities, already centres of commerce, also became important centres of learning. This was a development of the greatest importance for both Persia itself and the subsequent dissemination of Persian influence in Asia.

Since the Arab conquest in the seventh century, Arabic had been the language of religion and politics and it also came to be seen more widely as the language of learning. Scholars from Persia and elsewhere who descended on Baghdad would be expected to understand Arabic and to produce their work in that language. However, Persian was still widely spoken throughout Transoxiana, and as the caliphate became weaker so the Persian language gained ground in other spheres. While Arabic continued to retain its primary role as the language of Islam, Persian came to be used for a greater variety of purposes, and by the eleventh century it had largely regained an important role in the life of the people.[5] This was associated particularly with the rise of the Persian Saffarid and Samanid dynasties, which began the process of moving Persia away from the caliphate and reasserting its historic independence. Since the Samanids themselves came from Central Asia they always maintained a close association with it. This contributed to the importance that the area rapidly gained in the Persian world and its subsequent role in the dissemination of the wider aspects of Persian culture.

Following the initial Persian conquests, two distinct population groups were to be found in Central Asia. One of these consisted of the pastoral nomadic people, whose principal homeland was the steppe grassland. These people had over the millennia migrated southwards and attacked the sedentary civilizations of the Middle East. The most successful of them had established their own powerful states, which then dominated the region. The second major population group was that living in the cities of Transoxiana, centres of trade and industry, which had steadily built up their economic power. At times when the grip of the Persians over the region became weaker, the states centred in these cities were able to add to their political power. It was this process that resulted in the creation of the sultanate of Khwarazm in the twelfth century. This became a powerful state that was itself able to exert considerable influence throughout the region. At the same time as its political

Al-Balkhi (790–866), born in Balkh, astronomy

Al-Bukhari (870–?), born in Bukhara, writer

Abu Mashar [Albumasar]* (890–?), born in Balkh, mathematics

Al-Razi [Rhazes]* (865–925), medicine, chemistry, philosophy, astronomy

Al-Khwarizmi (863–901), born in Khwarizm, astronomy, geography (world map), algebra

Al-Farabi [Alpharabius]* (born in 870), from Wasij (Turkistan), science, geography, metaphysics

Al-Biruni (973–1048), born in Kath, astronomy, mathematics, geography (latitude and longitude)

Al-Jurjani (tenth century), born in Khwarizm, medicine, astronomy, mathematics

Al-Khujandi (tenth century) born in Khujand (Jaxartes), astronomy

Ibn Sina [Avicenna]* (970–1037), born in Bukhara, Ghazni 'Canon' encyclopaedia, medicine, geography, geology, philosophy

Khusrau (1003–1075), born in Balkh, geographer and explorer

Al-Farghani [Alfraganus]* (eleventh century), born in Farghana, geographer and astronomer

Omar Khayyam (1070–1123), born in Nishapur, poet (Rubaiyat), mathematician, astronomer

*Names by which these scientists and scholars would have been known in Europe

Scientists and scholars from Transoxiana and Central Asia listed in approximate chronological order of writings. Most of the work of these scholars was in Persian or, if in Arabic, would have been translated into Persian.

grip loosened, Persian cultural influences again increased and a great deal of the scholarly and scientific achievement of the Persian world was soon coming from this region.

In the early thirteenth century Transoxiana was invaded by the Mongols, the most powerful and aggressive people ever to come out of the heart of Asia, who rapidly gained control over most of the centre of the continent and much of the Middle East. Led by Genghis Khan, these pastoral nomads, whose homeland was to the south of Lake Baikal, created the largest empire to have existed up to that date anywhere in the world. At its maximum extent it stretched across the continent to include both Russia and China. After the death in 1234 of Ögedei, the son of Genghis Khan and the second Great Khan, the still growing empire became too unwieldy to be held together as a single unit. It soon split up into subsidiary khanates which themselves became semi-independent states. The main part of Transoxiana fell to Chagatai, another of the sons of Genghis Khan, and thanks to the Silk Road and its commercial cities it provided considerable wealth for its rulers.

The most important centre of Mongol power was China, and there they established themselves as a Chinese dynasty. However, by the middle of the fourteenth century the grip of the Mongols was beginning to weaken, and in 1368 the last of the Yuan (Mongol) emperors, Tögüs Temur, was forced back into exile in the old capital, Karakorum. While with the fall of the Yuan dynasty the most important centre of Mongol power had come to an end, for a time Mongol rule continued in certain places, including the khanate of Chagatai. The *Pax Mongolica*, the peace brought by the Mongols to the fractious tribes of Central Asia, had revived the Silk Road and for a time given considerable prosperity to Transoxiana. The possibility of the breakdown of this peace and a return to petty rivalries was not a welcome prospect.

This was one of the reasons for the widespread desire for the revival of the Mongol Empire, and it was responded to by a local warlord from near Samarkand. He was Timur Lenk, who had already established a power base for himself by becoming emir of Transoxiana. Better known in Europe as Tamerlane, or Tamburlaine, he proved to be a redoubtable warrior and was soon extending his conquests with vigour.[6] Timur was actually from the Turkish Barlas clan from near Fez to the south of Samarkand. He had, however, been educated in the Persian cultural tradition, which had suffused Transoxiana over the centuries. He was a Persian-speaker and had great respect for all aspects of Persian culture, something that was to become evident as his reign progressed.

In 1370, when news of the last Yuan emperor's death reached Transoxiana, Timur proclaimed himself successor to the fallen Chinggisids, the dynasty of Genghis Khan. From then on he considered that his principal task was to resurrect the Yuan Empire. He always proclaimed himself to be of Mongol-Turkish descent and in this way legitimized his claim as inheritor to the Chinggisid dynasty. He possessed a considerable appetite for conquest and power. Within ten years he had gained complete control over the Chagatai khanate, which became his base for further conquests. By 1390 he had conquered Persia itself, the historic centre of the great civilization that he so admired. During this conquest he is known to have paid a visit to Persepolis, where he would have been able to see the ruins of the ceremonial capital of the Achaemenids. In 1393 he captured Baghdad and occupied all Mesopotamia. As a result of this he had gained control over the principal centres of power in both the Persian Empire and the caliphate.

Unlike the previous Middle Eastern conquerors, who had moved their capitals to, or near to, Mesopotamia, from the outset Timur's centre of power lay in that other land of two rivers, Transoxiana – and so it remained. His capital was Samarkand, a city for which he always had the greatest affection and to which he regularly returned in order to recuperate after his many conquests. It was during these interludes that he began to embellish his favourite city with many fine buildings. In doing this he was certainly inspired by what he had seen elsewhere. It has even been suggested that his visit to Persepolis would have been an inspiration, although the ancient capital would then have been little more than a ruin in the sand. Important among those who thought so was Ruy Gonzáles de Clavijo, sent as ambassador to the court of Timur by King Henry III of Castile.[7] Based on the observations of Clavijo, John Ure expressed the opinion that 'When Tamerlane rode through Persepolis

Tomb of Rustum, near Shiraz.

he was not only making a symbolic triumphal progress but was, in all probability, making mental notes for more impressive triumphs at home based on what he saw here.'[8]

The Great Stairway is a veritable statement of empire in stone, considered by Forbis, as noted in Chapter Five, to have been 'a hand-chiselled filmstrip of obeisance to the emperor'.[9] If anything of it was to be seen by the time of Timur's visit, it would certainly have inspired the conqueror.

A great deal was known to the Elizabethans of the story of the Asiatic conqueror but, as with Cyrus, this would no doubt have been a mixture of truth and legend. Marlowe puts into the mouth of the conqueror the words: 'Is it not passing brave to be a King, / And ride in triumph through Persepolis?' (*Tamburlaine the Great*, II.5) But the new Persepolis was to be Samarkand, and Marlowe makes Tamburlaine's triumph outshine even Darius when he has him declaiming:

Then in my coach, like Saturn's royal son,
Mounted with shining chariot gilt with fire,
And drawn with princely eagles through the path
Pav'd with bright crystal and enchas'd with stars,
When all the gods stand gazing at his pomp,
So will I ride through Samarcanda streets. (IV.4)

Samarkand owed much to the Persian traditions of architecture from the Achaemenids to the Safavids. In designing the mosques, libraries and madrasas he built, architects were brought from as far afield as Shiraz, another city that seems to have particularly impressed him during his conquest. In the centre of his capital was the palace of Timur himself. The Gok Sarai – the Blue Palace – was highly fortified and around it were laid out many magnificent parks and gardens. One of Timur's favourite gardens was the Baghi Dilkusha, the Garden of Heart's Delight, which had been designed to commemorate his marriage to Tukal-khanum, the daughter of the khan. In 1404 Clavijo observed that Samarkand was a town set in the midst of a forest in which there were gardens and running water, fruit trees and cisterns, olive groves and aqueducts. As with the conquering kings of Persia, here another Persian-inspired conqueror created a paradise at the heart of his empire. It was, said Clavijo, 'the first of all the cities which he had conquered and the one that he had since ennobled above all others, by his buildings making it the treasure house of his conquests'.[10]

It is evident from the comments of such travellers that the city and its surroundings designed by Timur were very much in the tradition of the Persian *pairidaēza* dating from Achaemenid times. All the elements of this were clearly present, most significantly the vital running water that irrigated the land and enabled what had been ugly to become beautiful and what had been unproductive to become fruitful. At the centre of his paradise were his great buildings, including the palace and the mosques, to which the gardens would have been a magnificent backdrop and place of pleasure. Timur would undoubtedly have seen many such beautiful gardens during his conquests, and he brought back the architects and gardeners to recreate them in Samarkand.

As a result of all this frenetic activity of conquest interspersed with building, a new Persia was born in the heart of Transoxiana. The northwards displacement that had been observed over the centuries, and which had political, economic and cultural implications, reached its apogee with Timur and his successors. Despite his savagery towards his enemies, this Persian-speaking Turk was in many ways a cultured man who was most happy when engaged in discussions with scientists and scholars.

Samarkand was intended by Timur to be a city of beauty and culture, an oasis of tranquillity built with the spoils taken from other parts of his vast empire. It was not exactly to be a new Persepolis in the imperial sense but if, in Marlowe's words, Timur's 'native city Samarcanda' was to 'be famous through the furthest continents', it was to be a fame arising from the civilization rather than the power of his empire. However, he needed another capital for imperial purposes, and he chose to build this some 50 kilometres to the south of Samarkand. This was Shakhrisabz, formerly Kesh, in the territory

The dome of the Gur-Emir mosque from the eastern side, Samarkand, c. 1905.

The ruins of the 'White Palace' of Timur at Shakhrisabz, southern Uzbekistan.

of the Barlas clan. Timur is said to have asserted, 'Let he who doubts our power look upon our buildings' – and Shakhrisabz certainly was intended for this purpose.[11]

While Persepolis was a statement of both power and beauty in stone and in the *pairidaēza* that surrounded it, Timur chose to separate the power and beauty and to have one city displaying each. The two sides to the conqueror's character were evident in these two adjacent but very different Transoxianian cities. The one reflected his Turkish origins while the other reflected the Persian civilization he had adopted. According to Amin Maalouf, Samarkand 'was the most beautiful face the Earth has ever turned towards the sun'.[12]

In 1403 Timur returned to Samarkand after his abortive Indian campaign. The ruthless sack of Delhi left nothing, says Luc Kwanten in his book *Imperial Nomads*, but 'a trail of blood'.[13] Timur had also succeeded in defeating and humiliating the Ottoman sultan Bayazid. This event is central to Marlowe's *Tamburlaine* and to his depiction of Timur as the ruthless Asiatic conqueror. However, on his return, the other side of his character came to the fore and he threw himself into the further embellishment of his beloved city. We learn of 'feverish construction' in the capital, something that contrasted markedly with the destruction he had left behind elsewhere. Justin Marozzi, an English journalist, tells us that Timur's attention was then given almost obsessively to the completion of the glorification of his capital, 'with all the furious energy of war'. Marozzi called the Cathedral Mosque, which was one of Timur's final projects, 'the apotheosis of Timur's architectural creation'.[14] However, there was as yet no apotheosis of the old warrior's greed for territory, since the most important part of the old Mongol Empire still eluded him. This was China, and as the self-proclaimed successor to Genghis Khan, Timur was determined to conquer this country too. Consequently, in addition to all his building, he was also engaged in preparing for his next campaign. In 1405 he set out eastwards with an enormous army, but he was now 69 years old and in poor health. In January 1406 the conqueror of so many lands died in the ferocious Central Asian winter on the plain of Otrar, north of Tashkent. His body was brought back to his beloved Samarkand and there laid to rest in the Gur-Emir tomb prepared for him.

Timur's conquests did not long survive his death, and the Ottomans were soon able to regain their position as the leading power in the Middle East. The two capitals he had built in Transoxiana remained as twin memorials to his strange and ambivalent character. His love of cultural artefacts, mainly those of the Persian civilization, was indisputable. He was, said Grousset, not a barbarian 'but a cultivated man, a great lover of Persian literature and one who was always ready to quote the Koran'.[15]

It was to be the civilization of Samarkand rather than the power of Shakhrisabz that was to be Timur's most lasting legacy. Samarkand became one of the cities where his successors, the Timurids, created the most impressive ever indigenous civilization in Central Asia. Their achievements were firmly based on the heritage of that Persian civilization that had permeated Transoxiana for so many centuries and which had been espoused and passed on by Timur.

While the conqueror himself had brought little but death and destruction to India, among his successors were those who succeeded in bringing Persian influence of a very different kind to the subcontinent.

TWELVE

PARADISE OF BLISS: THE PERSIAN LEGACY IN INDIA FROM THE TIMURIDS TO THE MUGHALS

imur Lenk was a split personality in whom was combined a love of that Persian civilization he had inherited, and a ruthless desire for conquest and destruction. His twin and contradictory passions to create and to destroy did not fit together at all well. However, his successors, more educated and less violent than was the conqueror himself, inherited overwhelmingly the cultured and civilized side of his character. Very soon the great empire was lost and the inheritance of his successors, the Timurids, was to be measured in their artistic and intellectual achievements rather than their military conquests. What was left of Timur's empire centred on Transoxiana, the focus of the spread of Persian civilization into Central Asia.

Timur's son and successor, Shahrukh, was quite the opposite of his father and was said to have been of 'a cultured and pacific nature'.[1] He moved his capital well away from Samarkand to Herat, some 600 kilometres to the south, and left his son Ulugh Beg as viceroy of Transoxiana, known to the Arabs as Mawarannahr, with his capital in Samarkand. He may have done this to get away from Timur's centre of power, with all its violent associations, but under the old warrior's grandson, Ulugh Beg, things changed completely. His nearly half a century as viceroy and emir was a period of tranquillity and construction when the essentially Persian civilization of Central Asia flourished as never before. It was during the emirate of Ulugh Beg that some of the most magnificent buildings in

Shahrukh	1405–47, fourth son of Timur
Ulugh Beg	1409–49, grandson of Timur; Amir of Transoxiana; 1447–9, ruler of all the Timurid lands
Abdal-Latif	1449–51
Abu Said	1451–69
Husayn Bayqara	1470–1506

The most important Timurid rulers and their dates of rule.

Samarkand were built, including those around the Registan Square, regarded by Lord Curzon, who visited Samarkand during the later nineteenth century, as being 'the noblest public square in the world. I know of nothing in the East approaching it in massive simplicity and grandeur; and nothing in Europe . . . which can even aspire to enter the competition.'[2]

It was Ulugh Beg who arranged the interment of his grandfather in the beautiful Gur-Emir mausoleum close to the square. At this time, too, the magnificent gardens, which had converted Samarkand into that Persian paradise beloved by Timur, were further extended.

However, the most important achievements of Ulugh Beg were in the field of astronomy and mathematics. On the edge of his capital he built a splendid observatory in which astronomers were able to watch the heavens and do a great deal of research. Calculations of distances and orbits were made which later proved to have been remarkably accurate.

What was taking place in Timurid Transoxiana at the time of Shahrukh and his son Ulugh Beg was a most remarkable surge of new ideas in science, together with a flourishing of the arts. As a result the period of their reigns was the golden age of Timurid civilization. During the first half of the fifteenth century Transoxiana became one of the most important centres of scientific discovery in the world. In addition to astronomical research, the earth itself was not neglected, and maps were produced that displayed a surprising knowledge of geography – one was a worldview as seen from Samarkand, with the great city at its centre. This was all happening at a time when any serious scientific thought in the Christian world was being strongly discouraged by the Catholic Church. The omnipresent Christian *mappa mundi*, based on Catholic dogma and owing virtually nothing to real geography, inhibited any new ideas about the true nature of the world. What was happening in Transoxiana has been referred to as the 'Timurid renaissance', in which Samarkand together with its neighbour Bukhara and the capital city Herat became brilliant centres of a flourishing civilization. As in the time of Timur and his predecessors, this was fundamentally Persian, and the great traditions of that ancient civilization were once more transposed into Central Asia.[3] Visitors to the city at that time wrote of Samarkand being 'the mirror of the world', 'the garden of the blessed' or the 'fourth paradise'.[4] Samarkand and Bukhara became great centres of the arts and learning which, particularly in the fields of astronomy and geography, surpassed anything in Europe at that time.

It was Shahrukh and Ulugh Beg who together set the tone for the Timurid dynasty following the death of its founder, and their

Registan Square in Samarkand.

successors followed in their footsteps. They maintained an interest in the arts and sciences into the later years of the fifteenth century, when this great Persian-inspired civilization was disrupted by invaders from the north. These were the Uzbeks, and with their arrival this period of achievement came to an end. They captured Samarkand and forced the Timurids to retreat south, many of them even taking refuge in Afghanistan.

The resistance to these invaders was led by a Timurid prince called Babur, a direct descendant of Timur through his paternal grandfather. He was successful in regaining territory from the Uzbeks, even for a time retaking Samarkand itself. In 1512 Babur was defeated by the Uzbeks just north of Samarkand and was forced southwards, seeking refuge like so many others in Afghanistan. This marked the end of the Timurid dynasty and from this time on the Uzbeks became the rulers of Transoxiana.

Babur's centre of power was now Kabul, but he remained impatient to redeem himself by making new conquests. Historically, Afghanistan had been a holding area for successive invasions of India from the north and Babur, his homeland now conquered by the Uzbeks, was also forced to look to the south. In 1526 he invaded India using the Khyber Pass route into the Punjab. On the field of Panipat just north of Delhi, the site of many battles for the possession of India, he met and defeated the army of the sultanate of Delhi, which had for many centuries been the dominant power in the subcontinent. From there Babur moved on and occupied Delhi and Sikandrabad, the last capital of the sultanate. With this the sultanate came to an end and Babur was proclaimed emperor and established the Mughal dynasty, which was to rule over the greater part of India for the next three centuries.

Mughal derives from the Persian 'Mughul', meaning Mongol. Timur Lenk, the founder of the Timurid dynasty, had claimed to have Mongol blood and this claim gave legitimacy to his conquests as heir to the Mongol Empire. He married a Chinggisid princess and from then on always insisted on being known as 'gurgan', the Persian word for son-in-law, rather than khan. The link back to Timur continued through subsequent generations and the Mughals actually referred to themselves as Gurkhani. In so doing they perpetuated both their Timurid origins and their strong connections to Persian culture.

Successful as they were in battle, the military prowess of the Mughals was by no means truly representative of the nature of the new dynasty. They were, after all, successors to the Timurids and, like them, had both the desire and the capacity to create rather than to destroy. The early Mughals, at least, proved to be civilized rulers. They spoke Persian and were firmly in that great tradition of art, architecture, science and literature that had spread outwards from Persia via Transoxiana. As has been seen, the Persian expansion northwards had produced its own great scholars and scientists, such as Al-Biruni and Avicenna, the magnificent architecture of Samarkand and, of course, the *pairidaēza* that adorned their cities with parks and gardens. It was this civilization the Mughals brought with them that made them so much more than conquerors and added a whole new dimension to the art, architecture, literature and science of the Indian subcontinent.

It was Babur who began this process. Scion of the great Timurid civilization, he was said to be the most brilliant Asiatic prince of his age and, according to the British historian Vincent Arthur Smith, 'worthy of a high place among the sovereigns of any age or country'.[5] He wrote a diary, the *Babur-nama*, originally in Turkish

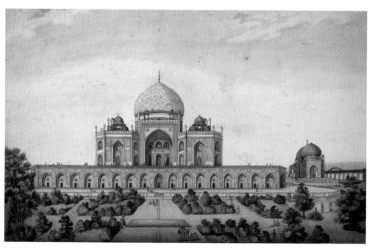

Mausoleum of Humayun in Delhi in 1820 surrounded by early Mughal gardens. Watercolour in Agra style by an unknown Delhi artist.

Miniature from Babur's *Waqiat-i-Baburi*, or *Babur-nama*, showing Babur laying out a garden in Kabul, *c.* 1508.

but translated into Persian after his death. In this he describes in detail his conquest of India and the nature of the new empire he inherited.[6] He did not have a very high opinion of India and saw it as merely a big land having such things as 'an abundance of gold and silver' and a huge and easily exploited workforce. He disliked the hot climate and missed the coolness and the mountain landscapes of Afghanistan. On his death in 1530 his body was taken back and buried in his beloved Kabul.

Babur was, like his ancestor Timur, both warrior and scholar, but he mercifully lacked the latter's savagery. His son Humayun was more completely in the Timurid tradition of Shahrukh and Ulugh Beg. Bookish and intellectual but an ineffective ruler, it was he who began the building programme that was to transform Delhi into

Babur	1526–30
Humayun	1530–56*
Akbar	1556–1605
Jahangir	1605–27
Shah Jahan	1637–58
Aurangzeb	1658–1707

*Humayun was faced with many rebellions during his reign and he was forced into exile between 1540 and 1545.

The first six great Mughals.

a splendid Mughal city. He was the first Mughal emperor to be buried in India, his tomb in Delhi being an early and magnificent example of that unmistakable Mughal architecture that derived via Transoxiana from Persia. It was designed by a Persian architect from Bukhara and was typical of both Timurid Samarkand and Safavid Persia.

Another Persian import was the garden that surrounded the tomb and which set off its architectural splendour against a background of greenery. It was the first of those Mughal gardens that derived from the gardens of Samarkand and before that the Persian *pairidaēza*. Such gardens were among the most magnificent gifts bestowed by the Mughals on India.

Humayun's successor, Akbar, was perhaps the most successful of all the Mughal emperors in uniting and extending his dominions, but he also found time to engage in building, with a fury that in many ways resembled that of his ancestor Timur in Samarkand. It was he who built the great fort at Agra and then went on to build a new capital city at nearby Fatehpur Sikri, the City of Victory. This capital was not the centre of Mughal power for very long and perhaps was never intended to be. Like Persepolis, it was designed as a ceremonial city and in many ways it resembled the Achaemenid capital itself. Most significant was the fact that the site had been chosen for largely symbolic reasons, in this case with its strong links to religion.[7]

Like his forebears, Akbar was a Muslim but he was also interested in the other religions of India and brought together representatives of each of them in the great five-storey Panch Mahal. There religious discussions took place and new ideas were formulated. This led over time to the emergence of a new, eclectic state religion that centred on Akbar himself. This was *Dīn-i Ilāhī*, the Divine Religion, and with Akbar at its centre the Mughal Empire took on many of the characteristics of a theocratic state.[8] However, toleration was extended to the other religions of the empire and Akbar himself took part in Hindu celebrations. This closely resembled the sympathetic way in which Cyrus behaved towards the religions of his Achaemenid Empire. The record of the reign, the *Akbar-nama*, written in Persian, gives many instances both of Akbar's interest in religion and his attitude towards it.[9] It is interesting to note that despite this toleration, Islam, the religion of the Persians and the Timurids, came to be treated more harshly than the other religions.

Akbar did not actually remain in Fatehpur for very long. He soon left for Lahore and later in his reign returned to the Red Fort at Agra. Behind its gigantic walls he and his immediate successors were secure and it was from there that they planned their campaigns for further expansion of the empire to the south. Fatehpur Sikri remained a magnificent symbol of Mughal power but religion always remained at the heart of the project. The grandest building in the city was the Jama Masjid mosque, built on the plan of the great mosque in Mecca. By then Akbar had proclaimed himself imam, and in so doing became the religious as well as the political head of his empire.

The final great addition to Fatehpur Sikri in the last years of the reign typifies that binding together of state and religion. This was the Buland Darwaza, the 'Gate of Victory', a triumphal gateway added to the Jama Masjid mosque. The eclectic nature of Akbar's state religion is also made clear from the inscription above the entrance, which reads, 'Jesus, son of Mary, said, on whom be peace: the world is a bridge, pass over it but build no house upon it.' The image of the bridge, which can also be found elsewhere in Fatehpur, encapsulated the idea of the link between the divergent peoples and religions of the empire that Akbar strove throughout his reign to create.

While Fatehpur Sikri was in the Mughal architectural style, there were also considerable Hindu influences with strong political meanings. The concept of the bridge is certainly an idea that would have applied also to Cyrus with his policy of tolerance of the diversity of the peoples of his empire. Neither Cyrus nor Akbar tried to force an artificial unity on the peoples of their empires but allowed the existence of a natural diversity. *Dīn-i Ilāhī* was intended most particularly to be the religion of the Mughal dynasty in much the same ways as Zoroastrianism had been the religion of the Achaemenid dynasty.

Akbar died in 1605 and his son and successor, Jahangir, built his magnificent tomb nearby at Sikandarabad. Like that of Humayun, it is surrounded by a splendid formal garden in the Mughal style.

The concept of the *pairidaēza* went on to play an important role in the architectural projects of Shah Jahan, the grandson of Akbar. Perhaps the most magnificent of all is the Taj Mahal at Agra, a tomb complex built by Shah Jahan for his wife Mumtaz Mahal, who died at a young age. Its magnificent gardens integrated into the complex of tomb, mosque and residences are very much in the Persian tradition. Artists and craftsmen from Samarkand, Bukhara, Balkh and even Shiraz worked on the mosaics, calligraphy and sculpture. The architecture of the tomb was in that mature Mughal style which owed so much to Samarkand, and before that to the architecture of the Sasanians. Like his ancestors Timur in Samarkand and Akbar in Fatehpur, Shah Jahan is said to have thrown himself into the project with wild enthusiasm and lack of concern for the cost, which proved to be a considerable drain on the coffers of the state.

Having built this magnificent complex in Agra, Shah Jahan then made the momentous decision to return his capital to Delhi. Like his forebears, he was a natural builder and on the site of Delhi he built the entirely new city of Shahjahanabad, with its massive walls and impressive towers.[10] It was laid out in a grid pattern, bisected by the Chandni Chowk, a grand processional way. Its most important and impressive building was a second Red Fort, intended to be the imperial residence and centre of government. This palace-fortress was, like the fort at Agra, built of red sandstone and, like the Taj Mahal, it also contained much white marble.

The Taj Mahal at Agra with watercourse and gardens.

While it was certainly a symbol of power in stone, inside its formidable walls was revealed architecture of the greatest beauty. The
pivot of the Red Fort was the Diwan-i-Am, the Hall of Public
Audience, where the emperor dealt with matters of state in front of
his subjects. As the British arts writer Louise Nicholson put it, this
was 'the Mughal Empire's centre stage for displaying its greatest
pomp and ceremony'.[11] This again placed the Mughals in that tradition, dating back to the Achaemenids, of the display of power in
stone. Like the Great Stairway leading to the Gate of the Nations
and the Throne Room at Persepolis, the processional route down
the Chandni Chowk and through the Lahore Gate led impressively
to the presence of the emperor.

However, while the Diwan-i-Am was the place where power
was on display, the real centre of power lay hidden behind it in the
Diwan-i-Khas, the Hall of Private Audience where the emperor met
privately with his ministers and the really important decisions of
state were arrived at. The *pièce de résistance* in this diwan was the

magnificent Peacock Throne inlaid with the most precious stones and symbolizing both the magnificence and the power of the emperor. Both Shah Jahan and his throne were described by the visiting Frenchman François Bernier in the following words:

> The King appeared seated upon his throne, at the end of the great hall, in the most magnificent attire. His vest was of white and delicately flowered satin, with a silk and gold embroidery of the finest texture. The turban of gold cloth had an aigrette whose base was composed of diamonds (and) an Oriental topaz exhibiting a lustre like the sun . . . The throne was supported by six massy feet said to be of solid gold, sprinkled over with rubies, emeralds and diamonds. I cannot tell you with accuracy the number or value of this vast collection of precious stones, because no person may approach sufficiently near to reckon them.[12]

The Diwan-i-Am, Red Fort, Delhi.

That the heart of the Red Fort, and therefore the heart of the Mughal Empire, was also a private place of beauty and relaxation for the emperor and the court was made clear by the couplet by Khusrau inscribed in Persian on the wall above the throne: 'If on earth there be a paradise of bliss, / It is this, Oh! It is this! It is this!'

The Mughals remained great lovers of gardens, fountains, cascades and pools, and these were all to be found in the Red Fort surrounding the diwans and the other buildings, including the harem and the private quarters of the emperor. As the couplet suggests, these Mughal gardens were certainly *pairidaēza* in the Persian sense of the word, something that was readily acknowledged by the Mughals themselves. The gardens of the Fort were in the classic Persian *char-bagh* (four garden) style, enclosed by a wall and crossed by two watercourses dividing them into four parts. At the centre was a pool with fountains and cascades. In the dry climate of Delhi, these *pairidaēza* would have been as welcome as had been those created by the Achaemenids in Parsa 2,000 years earlier.

Persian was, of course, the language most used by the Mughal dynasty, and the memoirs of the Great Mughals were either written in or soon translated into that language. It was the official language of the Mughal Empire and remained so until the nineteenth century. Babur also brought Persian book illustration to India and Akbar encouraged the local artists to revive the tradition of Persian miniatures. The most important historian of the period was Abu'l Fazl, the writer of the *Akbar-nama*, a detailed account of the Great Mughal's reign. It was said that the lyrical beauty and descriptive quality of Abu'l Fazl's Persian challenged the Sanskrit of India's own scribes. Abu'l Fazl also wrote the *Ain-i-Akbari*, a kind of 'Domesday Book' of the empire and a work of immense length. Sanskrit works such as the *Bhagavad Gita* were also translated into Persian, thus helping to provide that unity in diversity that Akbar saw as being the most important unifying force for his empire. In reality this linguistic divide set the rulers apart from the ruled, much like the French-speaking Normans were set apart from their Anglo-Saxon subjects. This powerful Persian–Hindi linguistic and cultural divide remained until the end of the Mughal Empire in the nineteenth century and was one of the factors contributing to the failure of the Mughals to bring India under their rule.

Despite the lapse of time, there is a remarkable similarity between the Achaemenids and the Mughals. Cyrus sought to build his empire by cooperation and consent and was largely successful in achieving this. However, apart from Darius, his successors moved away from his methods and reverted to the more usual type of imperialism based on compulsion and fear. This was a major contributory factor in the eventual fall of the Achaemenids and the victory of Alexander. In like manner, the Mughal emperor Akbar attempted to unify his empire by gaining the consent and trust of his subjects while his successors reverted to harsher methods. As John Keay puts it, by the time of Shah Jahan, 'the outspoken animation of Akbar's symposia had given way to a more awesome ceremonial and a more exalted symbolism. Now the "King of the World" ethereally presided from sun-drenched verandahs of the whitest marble.' In the Red Fort, 'the ritual of Court and Council and the conventions of costume were set in stone'.[13] After Darius the Achaemenid Empire was also in many ways 'set in stone' and this was very much the case of the Mughal Empire under Shah Jahan's son and successor, Aurangzeb, whose cruelty and Islamic intransigence set the scene for its fall. By the end of his reign, Muslims and Hindus had never been further apart.

The strong Persian influence on the Mughals, which had lasted for 200 years, was soon to be followed by a very different sort of Persian intervention in the affairs of the subcontinent. Soon after the death of Aurangzeb in 1707, other invaders began to move onto the Indian scene. The most ferocious of these was the Persian Nadir Shah, who in 1739 invaded India through Afghanistan, the route of so many conquerors in the past. Defeating the Mughal army at Karnal, he occupied Delhi and set the seal on the approaching end of the empire that had ruled India for the previous 200 years. A latter-day Timur, and usurper of the throne, Nadir Shah engaged in an orgy of slaughter and destruction similar to Timur's attack on the city 300 years earlier. He returned to Persia rich with booty, including much gold and precious stones. Among the latter was the famous Koh-i-noor diamond that was eventually to find its way into the British Crown Jewels. Most significantly, he took with him back to Persia the Peacock Throne, which had since the reign of Shah Jahan been the symbol of Mughal power. Its removal symbolized the end of the effective power of the dynasty. From then on its emperors were for the most part mere shadows, pawns in the hands of adventurers. For the next half-century the empire existed in name only. This situation was expressed in another Persian couplet: 'Az Delhi to Palam / Badshahi Shah Alam' (From Delhi to Palam / Is the realm of the Shah Alam). Palam was just outside Delhi, and the couplet was intended to deride the emperor Shah Alam, whose writ extended little further than the edges of his capital city. In 1804 he placed himself under the protection of the British, and a new power was poised to take over the ruins of the Mughal Empire. In order to communicate with the Mughals, the British found that they needed a knowledge of Persian, and this was something they quickly began to acquire. It was this more than anything else that gave them access to the literature and history of a great civilization and added considerably to their knowledge and understanding of what came to be known as the 'East'.[14] This was of particular value as the British became heirs to the Mughals and strove to consolidate their own world empire.

When the Peacock Throne was taken by Nadir Shah back to his capital, its role changed from being the symbol of the Mughal emperors to the symbol of the empire of the shah of Persia. It came to be regularly used in the great ceremonies of state, including coronations, and from then on the term 'Peacock Throne' became a kind of synonym for Persian imperial power. Both the term and the throne itself remained in use until the deposition of the last shah and the establishment of the Islamic Republic, discussed in Chapter Fourteen.[15]

THIRTEEN

Cyrus with Golden Caviar: The Last Dynasty Salutes the First

The first great empire to dominate the ancient world astonishingly continued to survive as an empire in one form or another for 2,000 years. Iran was ruled by a shah in the middle of the first millennium BC, and in the twentieth century AD the ruler was still a shah. However, by the twentieth century the country's significance on the world scene had become much reduced. It was a dinosaur from the remote past, living among the great powers that had come into existence long after Iran had lost its own status as one. After the Second World War the last dynasty attempted to revive its power and in this attempt Persepolis, the purpose-built capital of the ancient empire, had one last part to play on the world stage. By the twentieth century the world had undergone massive changes since that city had been the ceremonial capital of the superpower of its time. In the 1970s the ruins of the old imperial city were brought briefly back to life for the purpose of commemorating, and even resurrecting, the Persian Empire of antiquity.

As has been seen, the first Persian Empire, the Achaemenid, had been the ancient world's greatest power for some 200 years. It dominated much of the eastern Mediterranean and the Middle East until its defeat by Alexander the Great in the fourth century BC. Following the subsequent Hellenistic period, during which Alexander's successors ruled, and the long Parthian interlude, the Persian Empire was revived under the Sasanid dynasty. This dynasty ruled until its defeat by the Arabs in the middle of the seventh century, after which Persia for a time lost its identity and became part of the Islamic caliphate. By the tenth century, Persia had once again regained its independence from the caliphate and from then on into modern times it remained an independent country. It did so under a number of dynasties, all of which claimed legitimacy through their relationship to earlier dynasties. However, Persia's importance was fast diminishing, and by the time of the Qajar dynasty in the nineteenth century the country was of little consequence in the world.

In the later nineteenth century this began to change as a result of two important developments. In 1859 the Suez Canal was opened and the major route between West and East, which for centuries had been around the Cape of Good Hope, returned to the Middle East. While at first this was of marginal importance to Persia, it meant that the geopolitical significance of the Middle East was considerably enhanced. The two principal world powers of the time, Great Britain and Russia, both had an interest in Persia as it became caught up in that global rivalry between the two known as the 'Great Game'. Britain was especially concerned with ensuring communications with India, and the geographical location of Persia meant that that country was bound to be strategically significant in any power struggle. The importance of Persia to Britain was particularly emphasized by Lord Curzon, the future viceroy of India, in his book *Persia and the Persian Question* (1892). According to Curzon, the once-great empire had been reduced to 'one of the pieces on a chessboard' in the game being played out by Britain and Russia.[1]

The second development to change Persia's role in the late nineteenth-century world was the invention of the internal combustion engine and the need to search for supplies of oil to fuel it. It was discovered that Persia, like many other parts of the Middle East, was rich in oil, and this added further to the interest in the country.[2]

By the end of the First World War, the British Empire was at its apogee and its influence throughout the Middle East was paramount. The British interest in Persia had become so overwhelming that Morgan Shuster, the American representative to the Persian government, talked of the 'strangling' of the country, and later wrote a book on that subject. In it he maintained that Persia had become an 'unofficial mandate', and that its own government had very little say in its affairs.

It was in these difficult circumstances that the final dynasty, the Pahlavi, came to power. In 1921 Reza Khan, a general in the Persian army, became the minister of war, and his success led to his being appointed prime minister. He saw one of his main tasks as being to throw off foreign control and to reassert Persian power. The Qajar dynasty being by this time in a highly weakened state, and the shah being completely ineffective, Reza Khan was offered the crown. This he accepted, and the last of the Qajars, Ahmad Shah, was deposed and sent into exile. Reza Khan then chose the name Pahlavi, in this way linking his new dynasty to Persia's history and culture.[3] He was crowned Reza Shah Pahlavi in 1926 and a hastily assembled constituent assembly proclaimed him to be the *Shahanshah-i-Iran*. He proved highly successful in diminishing foreign, and in particular British, influence on the country, for which Shuster's *The Strangling of Persia* proved to be a book of considerable importance in pointing out new directions of policy.[4]

Reza Shah wished to associate his new dynasty with the pre-Islamic Persian past and especially the great age of the Achaemenids. However, at the same time he saw that if Persia was to regain any of its lost glory there also had to be modernization. In order to achieve this he undertook a radical programme of Westernization, including the secularization of the legal system. A new civil code, based on that of France, came into being and state courts replaced Islamic courts. Islamic sharia law and the influence of the clergy were both considerably curtailed and the traditional religious ritual of Ashura, on the tenth day of the month of Muharram, commemorating the martyrdom of Husayn, was abolished. In addition to this a new system of secular state schools came into being in which all instruction was in the Persian language, and Arabic words and names were removed. Persian history, with particular reference to the imperial past, took preference over Islamic instruction. The Persian solar calendar was brought back, replacing the Islamic lunar calendar. European dress was made mandatory and the veil was banned. This all went alongside the

Early portrait of Naser al-Din Shah (*r.* 1848–96).

emancipation of women, who had been forced to wear the veil and had been largely kept out of public life. Higher education was also catered for and a new national university was founded in Tehran. Alongside this was the Farhangestan-e Iran, the Academy of Persian Language, which was given the task of purifying the Persian language and removing foreign words. After so many centuries of linguistic interaction, the removal of Arabic words proved an immense task.

In Tehran, a Persian National Bank was established. This issued the national currency, the rial, and had the responsibility of conducting the country's financial policy. The bank also had a great deal to do with the economic policy of the country and finance was made available for improvements to the communications system and the establishment of new factories for the processing of agricultural products such as sugar and cotton. In 1933 the treaty between the Anglo-Persian Oil Company and the government was renegotiated, and the resulting increase in revenues from oil further contributed to the country's modernization.

As a kind of symbolic culmination of all these reforms and economic developments, in 1938 the name of the country was officially changed from Persia to Iran. This latter name had actually been in use since early times and derived from the Sanskrit *ārya*, meaning noble or highborn. The name had been given to the racial group that had moved during the first millennium BC from the centre of Asia into its peripheries and had usually attained positions of dominance in them. Many of the kings had been crowned *Shahanshah-i-Iran*, although variants on the name Persia, deriving from Pars or Fars, had also been used and had been most usually the ones used by Europeans. The Persians were proud of being members of the Aryan racial group, a fact that was used to add to the illustrious heritage that the shah was attempting to present to his people and to the world. The 1930s were, of course, a period during which racialism had become a highly influential concept in Europe, and by making Iran the official name, the shah was very much in tune with a prevalent idea of the time.[5]

This root and branch modernization and secularization was very similar to that which was happening at the same time in adjacent Turkey under Mustafa Kemal Atatürk. There the transformation was taking place from the Sunni Ottoman Empire into the secular Turkish national state.

Reza Shah greatly admired the Turkish leader. He paid visits to that country and followed the Turkish model whenever he considered it appropriate to do so. However, there were a number of significant ways in which the shah's regime differed from that of Atatürk. One was that while Atatürk had removed the Ottoman dynasty and established a republic in its place, Reza Shah looked back nostalgically to the Achaemenids and saw their empire as being the model for the revival of greatness. Again, while changes were brought about to purify the language, in particular removing Arabic words, the script was not changed as in Turkey, which had abolished the Arabic script and introduced the Latin script.

The most ominous difference was that in the Second World War, Reza Shah favoured the German side. The racialism associated with the change in the country's official name made him sympathetic to the Nazis and their policies. Because of this, pressure brought about by the British and Russians, who had considerable influence in Iran, led to his forced abdication in 1941 in favour of his young son, Mohammad Reza. The new shah had shown himself to be more inclined towards Britain and Russia and his father's abdication demonstrated the reality of world power in the middle of the twentieth century. The young heir accepted his new role, realizing the necessity of remaining firmly on the side of the Allied powers if he wanted to avoid the fate of his father.

In 1943 the first conference of the 'Big Three' – the Soviet Union, Britain and the United States – took place and Tehran was chosen as the host city. The first draft of the new post-war world order thus came into existence in the Iranian capital. While the shah was officially the host for this momentous event, his role was really little more than that of a spectator, and this made it abundantly clear to the young monarch how insignificant his country had really become. Tehran was merely a convenient meeting place and it was this that sowed the seeds in the mind of the shah about returning his country to its former glory.

While in the years following the end of the war Iran remained under the influence of the great powers, a strong nationalist movement arose that succeeded in moving the country into a more independent position. This centred on the left-wing Tudeh (Masses) Party, but there were in addition various shades of nationalists and anti-monarchists with their own particular agendas. These were brought together in a coalition by the formation of the National Front led by the veteran politician Mohammad Mossadeq. This called for the nationalization of the Anglo-Iranian Oil Company

Shahyad Tower, now the Azadi Tower, Tehran.

and for greater independence from Britain and the other Western powers. In this situation, violence increased, prime minister Haj Ali Razmara was assassinated, and the shah attempted to placate the nationalists by appointing Mossadeq prime minister. The central policy of Mossadeq's government was to take charge of the country's oil production. The Anglo-Iranian Oil Company was nationalized and the National Iranian Oil Company came into being in its place. This initially did much harm to the country's economy as the British severed diplomatic relations and called for a boycott of Iranian oil imports. Once more there was considerable political destabilization and the shah, having dismissed Mossadeq and appointed a right-wing successor, was forced to leave the country. In 1953 he returned, having secured the support of the army. Mossadeq was arrested and convicted of treason and the new administration proceeded to soften the Iranian stance. This suited the British, and the shah now presided over a period of considerable economic success.

However, at the same time the shah continued to dream of reviving the glories of ancient Persia and its Aryan past and saw further economic development as an important step towards achieving this end. In the 1970s he founded Rastakhiz, the National Resurrection Party, which was dedicated specifically to the revival of the greatness of Iran. In reality it did little more than applaud the actions and policies of the shah. At the same time, during the years of the Cold War, the shah continued to maintain a close relationship with the West, and this ensured that he continued to receive the military aid from the United States that helped build up his powerful armed forces.

By the 1960s, the idea of the revival of past greatness seemed to have completely taken over the shah's mind and the pressing needs of the economy came to be increasingly neglected. The shah stressed the continuity of Persian history and even attempted to trace a tenuous relationship between the Pahlavi and the Achaemenid dynasties. As the centrepiece of this upsurge of national pride it was decided to hold a great celebration of the 2,500th anniversary of the foundation of the Persian Empire by Cyrus the Great. The year 1971, the date chosen for this, seems to have been quite arbitrary, but it was accepted and the preparations went ahead. The intention of the shah was to demonstrate to the Iranian people and to the world at large the heritage of the country and the role his dynasty was playing in its preservation. Resurrection was certainly at the heart of what the shah had in mind for his country.

In Tehran great preparations were made, including the placing of bas-reliefs with ancient Persian themes in prominent sites across the city. Most important was the construction of an enormous tower incorporating an archway as a symbol of the whole event. This was the Shahyad Tower, meaning 'Souvenir of the Shah Tower'. Inside was an extensive display of precious artefacts illustrating the history of Iran since early times. The vast structure was located at the end of a grand avenue leading from the centre of the city. In this spectacular position it was intended to be the main symbol of the empire and an impressive focus for great events in the capital.

The *pièce de résistance* of the events was planned to take place in the ancient capital itself. Although by the nineteenth century the city was lost in the sand, the name Persepolis had remained down the centuries as an evocative symbol of power. Christopher Marlowe's play about Timur Lenk, who came to symbolize the fearsome power of the East, recalls Persepolis's glory when the conqueror proclaims that his ultimate wish was to take the city as Alexander had done over a millennium before.

There was also to be a role for Pasagardae, where the impressive tomb of Cyrus the Great still stood in lonely isolation on the plain north of Persepolis. In his address at the tomb the shah expressed his conviction that:

> After the passage of twenty-five centuries, the Iranian flag is flying today as triumphantly as it flew in thy glorious age. The name of Iran today evokes as much respect throughout the world as it did in thy days. Today, as in thy age, Iran bears the message of liberty and the love of mankind in a troubled world, and is the guardian of the loftiest human aspirations. The torch thou kindledst has for two thousand five hundred years never died in spite of the storms of history. Today it casts its light upon this land more brightly than ever and, as in thy time, its brilliance spreads far beyond the boundaries of Iran.[6]

The speech of the shah concluded with the exhortation, 'Sleep, O Cyrus, for we are awake.' By using such words as 'triumphant', 'respect', 'aspiration' and 'liberty', the shah was placing modern Iran directly in the lineage of Cyrus the Great and the manifold achievements of the Achaemenids, attempting to re-create a long-gone great power and to place it firmly among the powers of the present.

It cannot be denied that the great celebrations that took place in Persepolis in the summer of 1971 were spectacular. The ruined city once more had its brief moment in the global spotlight. Large numbers of heads of state, with the monarchs being given pride of place, were invited, together with ambassadors and other high officials, and huge tents were put up to accommodate the guests for the lavish banquet that was to be the centre of the event. A history of it all gives some flavour of the excessive lengths to which the shah went in providing luxurious food and drink for his guests:

In the sparkling light of huge crystal chandeliers, hung from a ceiling of pure silk, six hundred guests drawn from royalty and the world's executive power sat down together for a five hour banquet of the century . . . Chef Max Blouet of Maxim's de Paris had created . . . such minor triumphs as quail eggs stuffed with the golden caviar of the Caspian Sea, saddle of lamb with truffles (and) roast peacock stuffed with foie gras capped by its own brilliant plumage . . . There were some 25,000 bottles of wine.[7]

If the last statistic is correct, this would have been about forty bottles of wine per guest. The only thing in the banquet actually to have come from Iran was the golden caviar from the Caspian. One wag is said to have asked, 'Why, if we had 2,500 years of such great civilization, was almost all the food French?' It is significant that the French president Georges Pompidou was unable to attend. A number of other heads of state, including Queen Elizabeth II, also made their apologies.

Throughout the proceedings, the emphasis was always more on Cyrus than on Darius, who had actually built Persepolis, and the shah announced that the Iranian calendar was to be changed, with Year One being the date of the accession of Cyrus. The Cylinder of Cyrus, on which were itemized many of the deeds of the great monarch, became one of the emblems of the extravagant celebration.

After the banquet was over, the ruins of Persepolis became the backdrop for great processions of Iranian soldiers dressed in the uniforms of ancient Medes and Persians. The continuity of Iranian history was the underlying theme and the link between the remote past and the present was stressed. The feeling was engendered that day 'that the departed shades of the former lords of Asia were hovering unseen over the stage of their former glory'.[8] However, to Michael Axworthy it was all *folie de grandeur* on a sublime scale.[9] Certainly it was like Hollywood at its most extravagant. The narrator of the official film of the event was Orson Welles, who declaimed that this was 'Persia on parade'. Significantly, in this film the country was once more called Persia, rather than Iran.

The old name was deemed to be more appropriate in evoking the link with the past.

The shah gave another speech, 'before the shades of his adopted ancestors', as Paul Kriwaczek put it. In it he again emphasized the continuity with the ancient Achaemenid Empire and proclaimed the rebirth of Persian greatness. Once more he invoked the greatness of 'Cyrus, Great King, King of Kings' and repeated his assurance to the ancient ruler to 'Sleep, O Cyrus, for we are awake'.[10]

By this time the shah had become totally intoxicated by the whole project and what it represented and was far more concerned with linking himself and his dynasty to the glorious past than with the welfare of his people. However, none of this pomp and display could save the Pahlavis. Rather than covering the dynasty in borrowed glory, as had been intended, it actually increased the dissatisfaction of the Iranian people with their monarch. The summer of festivities emptied the exchequer, further weakened the economy and put the shah's relationship with his people under ever greater strain.[11]

Meanwhile, Iran was showing little sign of regaining any of that former glory for which the shah yearned. He attempted to address

Pasargadae, Iran: Iranian troops in ancient dress take part in the ceremonies before world royalty and heads of state commemorating the 2,500th anniversary of monarchy in Iran.

The shah enthroned in the ancient ruins of Persepolis, 1971, during the celebrations of the 2500th anniversary of the founding of the Persian Empire.

the situation by giving more power to the Majlis – parliament – and bringing about a number of reforms. However, the situation in the country failed to improve and it became clear throughout the 1970s that the Pahlavi regime was becoming ever more out of touch with the people. While in 1943 the shah had, at first at least, imagined he was playing host to his equals at the Tehran Conference of the 'Big Three', by the 1970s the reality was that his country was becoming ever more reliant on American support. For the U.S. the main use of Iran was as a buffer state against the Soviet Union, and for this to be effective the country had to be stable.

The restiveness among the population put this stability more and more into question and out of the increasingly difficult situation came a resurgence of Islam. This religion had been marginalized by both the shah and his father before him and had played little part in the shah's great schemes. The Shia Muharram commemorations and others had been banned by Reza Shah, but at the beginning of Muharram in 1978 there was an outbreak of violent demonstrations against the shah's government. On 11 December, the day of Ashura itself, there was a massive demonstration in Tehran and it became clear that the shah would not be able to control the situation for long. In January 1979, as Iran slipped into a situation of complete chaos, Mohammad Reza Pahlavi was forced into an inglorious exile and the dynasty – the self-proclaimed heir to two and a half millennia of greatness – was toppled.

The attempt by the shah to resurrect a long-vanished empire was in many ways the last vainglorious gasp of traditional imperialism deriving from ancient dynasties. Ironically, the reality of power in the twentieth century could have been foreseen as early as the Tehran Conference of 1943. Although this took place in his capital, the shah had been almost completely ignored throughout. His subsequent attempt to demonstrate the greatness of his country before the world proved to be illusory and in many ways embarrassingly laughable. After little more than half a century in power the Pahlavis were replaced by a regime that returned the country to Islam and embarked on an attempt to rebuild the nation's power using very different methods.

FOURTEEN
FROM SHAHYAD TO AZADI: THE ISLAMIC REPUBLIC AND THE ANCIENT LEGACY

T he last shah left Iran in January 1979 on what was officially an extended holiday but one from which he was never to return. He died of cancer in Egypt just six months later. The Ayatollah Khomeini, exiled by the shah for his subversive activities, returned by plane on 1 February from Paris, where he had spent the final years of his exile.

His return was almost messianic and there were cries of 'Imam amad', 'the Imam has come'. He was accepted immediately and without question as the de facto ruler of the country. The army defected from the shah to the new regime and revolutionary committees were established throughout the country. The Shia religious establishment now assumed power, and a Revolutionary Council dominated by clerics was formed. In effect the Holy City of Qom, long the main centre of opposition to the regime of the shah, took over from the secular city of Tehran. The anti-clericalism of the shah's regime died a rapid death and there was little opposition to the return of Islam and Islamic ideas. In March there was a referendum on the form of government that should replace that of the shah, and a vote of 97 per cent was recorded for the establishment of an Islamic Republic.

In October a new constitution was drafted, the main theme of which was 'dual control' by the civilian and clerical institutions. The Majlis was to be elected by popular vote while the Guardian Council was made up of clerics and was an appointed body. The president was to be elected by popular vote and there was also a dominating figure to be known as the 'supreme leader', the first of whom was Khomeini himself. He had the ultimate power over everything in the country and could overrule both the president and the Majlis. Together with this he also assumed the role of *Vilayat-e Faqih*, Guardian of the Law, which also made him in effect the moral supervisor of the nation. Later on in his period of office the Ayatollah established his own 'Expediency Council', also called the 'Council for the Discernment of State Interests', which he appointed and chaired and in which the most important decisions were taken and ratified.

In January 1980 Abol-Hassan Bani-Sadr, a socialist, was elected to be the first president of the Islamic Republic of Iran. The new government then moved fast to bring about fundamental changes in virtually every sphere of the country's life. Islamic dress and other codes were re-imposed and the civil courts were put under the control of the clergy. They proceeded to bring back sharia – Islamic law – and to enforce this throughout the country. The economy was put firmly under state control and the foreigners who had been so influential were ousted. The oil industry was re-nationalized and the newly established Iranian National Oil Company took charge of all oil production in the country. All other foreign interests in the country, which had become considerable under the shah, were expropriated. The new republic was becoming a theocracy with firm state control and the supreme power was ultimately in the hands of one man. The weakness of the shah had within a year been replaced by the strength of the Imam Khomeini.

There were nevertheless at first deep divisions in the leadership and much opposition to Khomeini himself. The fiercest opposition came from the Mojahedin-e-Khalq, the People's Mojahedin (MEK), which had been a guerrilla movement at the time of the shah. It was Islamic but also Marxist and had the support of large numbers of young people and many students. Its aim was to establish a state that was more ideologically based than one which was run by clerics. The Mojahedin was detested by Khomeini and his supporters, and the conflict between the two produced considerable violence in the early years of the revolution. The left-wing president, Bani-Sadr, who had been a member of the Tudeh Party, had become closely associated with the Mojahedin and with their defeat by Khomeini, Bani-Sadr was forced to flee the country. He was replaced in late 1981 as president by Ali Khamenei, and the prime minister was Mir Hossein Mousavi. The influential speaker of the Majlis was Ali Akbar Hashemi-Rafsanjani, who was later to succeed Khamenei in the presidency.

This, together with the pre-eminence of Khomeini himself, set the scene for the balance of power in Iran in the 1980s and on into the 1990s. Khomeini saw Islam as being a religious ideology to replace Marxism, which was in its final stages. In this context, Khamene'i was increasingly regarded as being conservative, Mousavi as radical and Rafsanjani as being the moderate of the trio. However, to Patrick Clawson and Michael Rubin, in their book *Eternal Iran* (2005) this categorization was too simplistic and they described both Khamene'i and Mousavi as being hardliners while Rafsanjani was more inclined to cut deals and was described by them as being 'pragmatic'.[1]

While all these major leaders were in general agreement on the core programme of the revolution, their attitudes to both the Islamic and the pre-Islamic history of Iran were somewhat different. It is possible to talk in general terms of the 'hardline' and the more – at least relatively – 'liberal' wings of the Islamic state, and these attitudes determined the extent to which particularly pre-Islamic studies were allowed to continue and even to be encouraged. The particular character of Iran, and its historical and religious differences from the rest of the Islamic world, was from the outset fully recognized. However, considering the prime importance of Islam and matters relating to social and economic questions, archaeological and historical research was not in the first instance given any priority.

When revolutions take place and new regimes that promulgate new ideas and ideologies take charge, the past is usually then considered to be at best no longer worthy of much attention and at worst as having been thoroughly evil. In either case all signs of the existence of the past need to be expunged. When regimes such as the Bourbons in France and the Romanovs in Russia were toppled by violent revolutions, the process was regarded as the sweeping away of the waste of history.

However, there was a big difference between the aftermath of the removal of those European regimes and that of the removal of the Pahlavis. What replaced it was not a new ideology raring to be tried out but an ancient religion with a history going back well into the previous millennium. Rather than the past being swept away, what was happening was one past was being replaced by another. While the Achaemenid past had been used by the Pahlavis as justification for their actions, the Islamic past was now being used as justification for the new regime. Just as the shah had looked back for his inspiration to Cyrus, so Khomeini looked back for his to the Prophet Muhammad. While this produced something very different, it was something that was nevertheless fundamentally Iranian.

The Shia Islamic tradition had since the time of the last of the orthodox caliphs been embedded in the life of Iran. It was firmly based on the belief that the legitimacy of the caliphate was derived from the continuation of the bloodline of the Prophet in what was in effect a dynastic succession. This has been variously translated as being the 'household' of the Prophet or the Prophet's 'tribe'. The contention of the Shia was therefore that only members of the dynasty had the right to be the rulers of Islam and so should become the successors or caliphs. From the outset they considered that the caliphates of the Umayyads and Abbasids were illegitimate. The main Shia ritual centred on the martyrdom of the Prophet's grandson Husayn, the last of the orthodox caliphs, in the Holy Month of Muharram. An especial significance attached to the tenth of the month, Ashura, the day on which Husayn was murdered by agents of the Umayyads.

While this Shia belief had existed in Iran throughout its years of subjection to the caliphate, and later in the time of the invasions by the Turks and the Mongols, it was the Persian Safavids, the dynasty that restored the country's independence, who had in 1501 first made Shia the official national religion. As a consequence, the Safavids were regarded by the Islamic Republic as being the model for what was now happening. The leader of the movement to reinvigorate the Shia was Mujtaba Mirlawhi, who established the Fida'iyan-i Islam – the Devotees of Islam – after 1945. It was

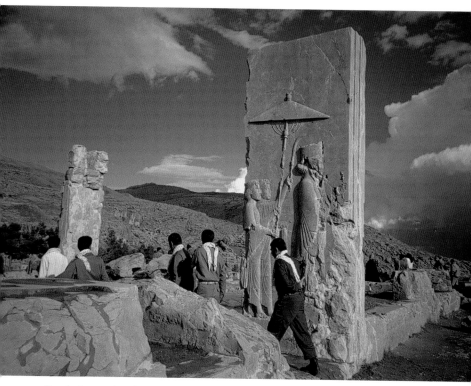

Revolutionary Guards visiting Persepolis, 2000.

he who stressed the role of the Safavid dynasty, taking the title of *Navvah-i Safavi* – the servant of the Safavis.

Looked at this way, Shia Islam can be regarded more than anything as a national or nationalist phenomenon, and this is clearly seen in its opposition to capitalism and to Western imperialism. Shia taught of the 'Hidden Imam' who would return and inaugurate an era of true Islamic government (see Chapter Ten). Khomeini developed this concept and was even considered by many of his followers to be himself the imam. The Islamic government he envisaged was firmly based on the teachings of the Koran and the correct interpretation of the Koran was thus seen as vital. This explains the importance of *Vilayat-e Faqih* to Khomeini. In his role of interpreter of the Islamic law he was able to adapt Islamic teaching to the modern world and to give it a social message. It was in this way that Shia Islam was converted into an ideology. In this,

Khomeini's mentor had been Ali Shariati, who maintained that Islam – not communism – was the answer to the evils of capitalism. Shariati went further and claimed that Islam had been twisted by the clergy into a dogma, while it was really an ideology. This linked it into the idea of the 'Third World' and to opposition to the West, in particular to America, which became 'The Great Satan'. Shia Islam continued to develop in this way during the 1970s at a time when the ideology of communism was on the wane. When Khomeini began to adapt the religion to the conditions of Iran in the 1980s the country's proletariat found it more attractive than either socialism or communism, and Islam was able to take on the role of ideology with little difficulty.

Far from rejecting the past in the traditional revolutionary manner, the Islamic Republic built its new Iran on its own Islamic past. This looked back to the Safavids not as the creators of Shia Iran but as the bridge between the early years of Islam and the modern era. As a result of this Islamic emphasis in the early 1980s, it would have seemed that the pre-Islamic, and particularly Achaemenid, past was to have received the same treatment as the Bourbons and the Romanovs: to be condemned and then forgotten as an ancient irrelevance. However, this was far from being the case and in the new Iran the ancient empire was from the outset accorded a place of honour.

At first this may not have seemed to be the case, as archaeological and other work in Persepolis and its surroundings was brought to a halt. Since it was the Safavid dynasty to which the new Shia establishment looked as their Islamic forebears, the ancient civilization was certainly not their first priority. Already by 1979 the physical evidence of the great ceremonies that had taken place in Persepolis at the beginning of the decade was fast falling to pieces. What had been referred to as being a second 'Field of the Cloth of Gold' was already fast disappearing into the sands. This situation then continued on into the 1980s. However, while there was at first little attention paid to the centre of the ancient empire, there was certainly no Alexandrian bout of destruction either. The graven images of Zoroastrian times were just ignored. The few visitors to Persepolis and Pasargadae during the early years of the

Islamic Republic speak of the way in which the ancient sites lay deserted rather than desecrated, and appeared to be returning to the sands from which they had been rescued by archaeologists in the nineteenth century. However, what was happening was largely about prioritizing the Islamic credentials of the new regime, rather than a deliberate attempt to ignore or destroy the country's pre-Islamic past. The retention of that all-important national identity was always seen as essential to the proper understanding of the nation and its past.

The particular significance of Pars as being where Iran had first come into existence had always been recognized and the region had consequently been accorded a special place in historical studies. The importance of the Achaemenid dynasty, which had begun its rise to power in Pars, had also made the province the accepted core region of the Persian state. The fact that this was also recognized by the new regime can be seen from the establishment in the 1980s of a Foundation for the Study of Pars based in Shiraz. This foundation was closely associated with the University of Shiraz and was concerned mainly with historical and archaeological research. This indicated in many ways a continuation of the recognition of the special position accorded the province by the Pahlavis. The principal work of the foundation has been archaeological and it has produced a number of articles and research papers. Since this work by the foundation would have had to receive official approval from Tehran, this gives some indication of how the history of ancient Persia was viewed by the new regime once it had established itself.

A book on Pars written by Koorosh-e Sarvestani and published by the foundation identifies 'a people who called themselves Aryans' emigrating from Central Asia southwards into Pars.[2] They spoke dialects of what was essentially the same language. They called their land 'Arya Waich' – the country of the Aryans – and called their language *E'ran shatra*, which evolved into 'Iran Shahr'. Cyrus II, the founder of the Achaemenid dynasty, is referred to as being 'Cyrus the Great' and it is stated that he 'established the greatest empire of the time by his remarkable deeds'. He was 'considered by historians to be a sagacious and competent king and was deemed

Zolqarnein (possessor of two centuries) by great scholars'. The use of the term 'possessor of two centuries' here is intended to indicate the influence that the deeds of Cyrus, who reigned for some thirty years, continued to exert throughout virtually the entire Achaemenid era.

Sarvestani's book goes on to examine the pre-Islamic religion of Zoroastrianism in some detail. It is described as having been a monotheistic religion, worshipping 'a matchless and great god called Oromazes'. It is also contended that after the fall of the Achaemenids, Pars was the only territory where what are referred to as 'true Zoroastrianism and its holy scriptures' were preserved. It was Ardashir I, founder of the Sasanid dynasty, who then restored the religion in Pars and throughout the country. This all suggests quite a positive and even benign attitude towards the religion that had preceded Islam. The worship of Zoroastrianism was permitted and it received protection from the Islamic Republic.

Sarvestani continues with an account of the Islamic period with particular reference to Pars, contending that 'Farsees have always been in deep sympathy with the Prophet's household'. He relates how the first Iranian to go in search of the Prophet was Salman-e Farsi, a man whom the Prophet is said to have referred to as 'one of our household'. In his *Fars-nama*, Ibn Balkhi wrote that the people of Pars have been named the *Ahrar-ol-Fars*, the Free Men of Fars. According to Balkhi, the Prophet said, 'God chose two groups from among the people, Qoreish from the Arabs and Parsees from Ajams'.[3] This all elevated Pars to a very special position in Islam. It was seen as being, in effect, the Hejaz of Iran, the place where Islam had first taken root in the country.

By the time the Islamic Republic was firmly established, Pars was thus being accorded a unique historical role. It was there that both the Achaemenid Empire and Iranian Islam had originated, and its holy shrines 'have always won Fars the reverence of lovers of the Prophet's household and the Shi'ites of the world'. It has remained, according to Sarvestani, 'in the vanguard of the preservation and development of the holy values of the Revolution'.[4] In this way, by the 1990s under the Islamic Republic, the ancient and the contemporary worlds were brought together geographically in

Pars, which was recognized as being the heart of what had been essentially Iranian since ancient times.

Scholars outside Iran have also emphasized the particular Iranian contribution to the nature of Islam. The Islamic scholar Patricia Crone made a study of the importance of the native Persian prophets of early Islam and how they shaped the way in which the new religion developed in the country. Her book on the subject published in 2012 was very well received in Iran itself.

While the special position of Pars was recognized unequivocally by the Islamic Republic, attitudes to the Achaemenids themselves were often more ambivalent. This may at least partly have had something to do with the central role accorded to them by the discredited Pahlavis. At first the new rulers were wary of being too closely associated with these early rulers and saw the Shi'ite Safavids as being their real forebears.

During his time as president of the Republic, Ayatollah Khamene'i paid a visit to Persepolis and wrote the following judgement on his experience:

> In my visit . . . I witnessed two distinct attributes lying side by side. First, the art, elegance, and the superb ability that has created . . . monuments which, after the lapse of tens of centuries, still remain a marvel to mankind. On the other hand, next to it lies exploitation and brute force . . . an individually cruel greatness . . . one has become the ruler of many. This is the dark and bitter history of the exploited . . . We must recognise these monuments as a valuable treasury in which we can see history and humanity, Iran and the Iranians, together with their legacy. We must preserve them.[5]

The Ayatollah's visit and his reaction to what he saw demonstrated the importance not only of Persepolis but of Pars as a whole. This was the province in which the state had been founded and where its distinctiveness was most in evidence. There the country's Achaemenid beginnings were brought together with its Shia Islamic present. Lindsey Allen contended that the Khamene'i visit to Persepolis illustrated the 'qualified national pride surrounding a

The revolution came to Iran in 1979. The Shahyad Tower in the background
was renamed the Azadi (Freedom) Tower.

monument so clearly evoking the country's monarchic tradition.'[6]
The continuity that had been sought by successive rulers over the
ages was certainly 'monarchic' in this sense. Islamic Persia had
been transformed into Persian Islam, and the Iran/Persia heritage
was central to that individuality which over the centuries had made
the country so different from other Islamic countries. Lawrence
Paul Elwell-Sutton, an Islamic Studies scholar, observed that, 'Iran
had never been conquered spiritually, and had always in the end
absorbed her conquerors while retaining her own integrity.'[7]
Cyrus, Shah Abbas, Mohammad Reza Pahlavi and the Ayatollah
Khomeini, together with many other rulers, were very different in
their beliefs and aspirations but they all held in common a firm
belief in the role of their country. To Michael Axworthy, Iran was
an 'empire of the mind'. It is perhaps the continuity of this 'mind'
that in a fundamental way made Iran the longest-lasting imperial
state in world history.

Located in a prominent position in Tehran at the junction of
major roads is the triumphal arch in white stone, built in 1971 by the
last shah to celebrate the 2,500th anniversary of the Achaemenid
dynasty. It also acts as a grandiose gateway to the capital. On its
official opening it was named the Shahyad, which means 'souvenir of the shah', and it contained galleries filled with exhibits
connected to the monarchy and its history. Within a decade of the
events of 1971, the monarchy had been overthrown and replaced

by the Islamic Republic. However, far from being considered an undesirable relic of the former regime, the arch was retained. Its role in the new regime became a different one and it was renamed the Azadi – Freedom – Tower. It remains an impressive gateway to Tehran, but what had once been a symbol of the ancient empire was transformed into a symbol of the new Islamic Republic.

While neither Shahyad nor Azadi may have been particularly appropriate names for the arch, the unity of the vast monument symbolizes in stone that continuity over the millennia that has transcended the many different regimes that have ruled the country through the ages.

FIFTEEN

LOST IN TRANSLATION?

I n many ways the interactions between Persian and European culture over the centuries has been sporadic and somewhat limited. In large part this is due to the preponderance of Greek and Roman influences, which came about as the Roman Empire expanded westwards. This contributed also to bringing about the deep religious rift between Christianity and Islam. From this developed the 'East is East and West is West' concept that has already been touched upon.

In spite of this, European figures have been prominent in the exploration and dissemination of Persian culture from the late eighteenth century onwards. Sir William Jones (1746–1794), a judge in the supreme court in Calcutta, became acquainted with Persian through its use in India during the late Mughal period. He also learned Sanskrit, the ancient language used in religious and other early writings. From his studies he developed the idea that many of the languages spoken in Europe and those of adjacent Asia as far as northern India belong to one family of languages, which later became known as Aryan or Indo-European.[1] Jones himself went on to translate some Persian texts, such as the poetry of Hafez, into English, but credit for the new discoveries in philology must be shared by the Frenchman Abraham-Hyacinthe Anquetil Duperron, a contemporary of Jones who was also a researcher of Sanskrit and Persian. The rivalry and at times outright hostility between them is recounted by Paul Kriwaczek in his book *In Search of Zarathustra.*[2]

Similarly, in the field of archaeological discovery in Persia, Europeans were prominent. Figures such as Georg Friedrich

Grotefend and Sir Henry Rawlinson were central in recording and deciphering cuneiform inscriptions in such places as Persepolis, Pasargadae and Bīsitūn. Other travellers, many of them diplomats or other employees of European governments, did valuable work in sketching and recording the ancient sites they visited, as John Curtis recounts.[3] Their work formed a basis for the subsequent investigations of the Archaeological Service of Iran, carried out by such figures as Ali Sami and Ali Hakemi.

Among the world's most famous artefacts, the Ardabil Carpet is a product of the great flowering of the arts under the Safavid rulers of Iran, c. 1539–40.

Setting aside this kind of academic work, knowledge of Persian culture in the West was limited and selective. Rather than any in-depth concept, we come across random bits and pieces. For example, several composers touch on Persian themes, such as Schumann in *Paradise and the Peri* (1843), Rimsky-Korsakov in *Scheherazade* (1888) and Strauss in his tone poem *Also Sprach Zarathustra* (1896). Even Mozart in *The Magic Flute* (1791) recalls Zoroaster in the figure of the high priest, Sarastro.

Similarly in literature we know Omar Khayyam through Edward Fitzgerald's hugely popular, if not entirely accurate, translation of 1859, just as we know something of the tale of Rustam from the *Shahnameh* through Matthew Arnold's poem 'Sohrab and Rustum' (1853). Many other English writers, such as Thomas Moore, Robert Southey and William Beckford, also share this fascination with Persian and generally Oriental themes, which was echoed in the fashion for Persian carpets, textiles and costumes, always with the emphasis on the exotic and flamboyant. A general appreciation of the wealth of the Persian cultural tradition is more difficult to find.

The bulk of any written literature that might have existed before the Islamic invasion has been lost in successive attacks, such as those of Alexander and the Mongols. An exception is the Avesta, the sacred text of Zoroastrianism. Although the earliest version we know dates probably from the Sasanid period, it is proof of a much earlier body of myth of pre-Zoroastrian origin preserved in the oral tradition. Gods, heroes and fabulous creatures appear mostly in that section of the Avesta known as the Yasht. The Avesta was preserved in part because it was carried east into India by Zoroastrians escaping Islamic rule in Persia. They settled initially in Gujarat and became known as the Parsees.

Following the Islamic conquest in Persia itself, Persian, despite surviving as a spoken language, was largely overshadowed by Arabic in literary use. With customary Persian resilience, it was revived in the Sasanid period by poets such as Daqiqi, Rudaki and Ferdowsi. Ferdowsi's huge work in verse, the *Shahnameh*, relishes the Persian language and Persian traditions. It became the national epic and is still treasured by the Iranian people. It traces the history of the Persian kings back through known history and into the world of legend and myth. Interestingly some of the characters and tales of the *Shahnameh* appear also in the Avesta. An example is Gayomartan, the mythical first human being of the Avesta, who appears as Keyumars in the *Shahnameh*. Similarly, the character of Yima in the Avesta reappears in the *Shahnameh* as Jamshid, one of the most famous kings in Persian mythology. He is remembered as having ruled for 300 years in peace and harmony before overweening self-importance caused him to lose his Divine Glory (*farr-i izadi*). This opens the way for evil (Angra Mainyu or Ahriman) to appear in the form of the wicked Zahak, who has sold his soul to the devil. His victory over Jamshid brings about chaos in the world, and this same theme of the Divine Glory of kings and its loss through excessive pride and ambition runs through myth and legend into history. Returning to the *Shahnameh*, after the death of Jamshid there follows a period of turmoil between the kingdom of Turan (identified as being in Central Asia) and Iran (the western region), a conflict still recognizable in historical time, as we have already seen.

Involved in the mythical conflict are three generations of one family – Sam, the grandfather, Zal, the father, and Rustam, the greatest of all the heroes of the *Shahnameh*. The exploits of Rustam and his splendid horse Ruksh include crossing a huge arid desert and fighting with lions, dragons and other beasts. One episode familiar in English through Arnold's poem 'Sohrab and Rustum' involves Rustam being manoeuvred by the Afrasiyab, king of Turan, into combat against his own son, each being ignorant of the other's true identity. The scene where Rustam, having killed Sohrab, realizes that he has in fact killed his own son is still very much alive in Persian art and storytelling.

Throughout the *Shahnameh* the reader will recognize familiar motifs from other mythologies. Rustam's adventures remind us of other heroes such as Hercules or Odysseus. Another familiar theme is that of a baby of high birth being abandoned by its family and brought up by an animal or by peasants before eventually being returned to its rightful place in society. Zal, Rustam's father, is brought up by the mythical bird Simurgh, and Cyrus, also abandoned, is fed by a dog before being adopted by a shepherd. We are reminded of

'Zal consults the Magi', from the *Shahnameh* of Shah Tahmasp, *c.* 1530–35.

Romulus and Remus being brought up by a wolf, or Shakespeare's
Perdita in *The Winter's Tale,* also saved by a shepherd.

Mythical threads like these, deriving from ancient oral traditions, have worked through into legend and subsequently into
what Roger Stevens calls 'para-history', where myth, legend and
reality become inextricably blurred.[4] Ferdowsi tells of the lives
and loves of real Sasanid kings like Khusrow II, who falls in love
with the beautiful Shirin. The story of the various setbacks in their
courtship before they finally marry is picked up by the later poet
Nizami Ganjavi in his *Khusrow va Shirin* (*c.* 1180). Alexander the
Great, as Iskander, appears in the *Shahnameh* as a rather ambiguous figure, half-heroic Persian prince with a legitimate claim to the
Divine Glory and a half-evil destructive usurper. Interestingly,
Cyrus the Great is not immediately recognizable in the *Shahnameh*,
but the story of Kay Khusrow, one of the mythical Kiyanian kings
in Ferdowsi, bears considerable resemblance to Herodotus' tale of
the birth and upbringing of Cyrus (Kurush) – enough, perhaps,
to indicate that they are one and the same person.

Many of the versions of the *Shahnameh*, in both prose and
poetry, were produced in various parts of Persian territory, but that
of Ferdowsi remains the most revered. Even travellers up to the
present day attest to its being a living part of the national culture.
Michael Wood in his BBC television series from 1997 on Alexander
the Great describes how professional storytellers (*naqqal*) still
perform parts of the *Shahnameh*.[5] A recent novel by Farnoosh
Moshiri, *The Drum Tower*, although set in the period of the Islamic
Revolution, is enriched by the symbolic use of the mythical bird,
the Simurgh.[6]

Poetry was highly prized by both the Persians and the Arabs.
True to their skill of learning from other cultures, Persian poets
from the ninth and tenth centuries onwards wrote poetry in the
Persian language, but often adapted Arabic forms and metres to
suit their purpose. As well as the *masnavi* form used by Ferdawsi,
they also developed the *qasida*, often utilized by courtly poets to
write poems of praise for the various caliphs who were their patrons.
The *ghazal* is a shorter lyric form used often to express love, both
sacred and human. This form flourished in the thirteenth and early

fourteenth centuries, a period often described as the golden age of Persian poetry, surprisingly perhaps in that it coincides with the terrible invasion by the Mongols. Interwoven with expressions of love, works by poets such as Sa'di (d. 1292), Rumi (d. 1273) and Hafez (d. 1389) are philosophical musings on beauty and the fragility of human life. In some ways reminiscent of the Japanese haiku, *ghazals* are not easy to replicate and there has been a tendency by translators to overdo the more exotic elements – wine, roses, nightingales and so on – and play down the philosophical element. Another form of poetry, the *rubais*, or quatrain, became famous in English literature through Edward Fitzgerald's version of the *Rubáiyát of Omar Khayyám* in the late nineteenth century, which became immensely popular. While it may not be a very accurate translation, it served to introduce English readers to the twelfth-century Persian poet, and at the same time heightened the perception of anything Persian being flamboyant and exotic. This same impression was reinforced by many translations into European languages of *The Thousand and One Nights*, a collection of tales written down in Arabic but incorporating stories from many sources, primarily Arabic, Persian and possibly Indian. Such sources are inevitably difficult to identify with any certainty, but the framework of the collection is almost definitely Persian in origin. It concerns a king who kills each of his successive wives on the morning after the consummation of their marriage, until he eventually marries the clever Scheherazade, a vizier's daughter. She avoids death by captivating the king each night with a story, interrupting the narrative every time at a critical point and postponing the denouement until the next night. There are references in Arabic sources to a translation, possibly as far back as the tenth century, of a Persian book, since lost, called *Hazar Afsaneh* (A Thousand Tales). Muhsin Mahdi has attempted to re-establish this lost archetype in his *Alf Layla wa-Layla* (1984). Certainly, various versions of the tales became widespread in Europe from the time of Antoine Galland's translation into French in the early eighteenth century. English versions followed, the most famous perhaps that by Sir Richard Burton in the late nineteenth century. Its self-conscious audacity and exotic eccentricity necessitated its private publication in order to avoid prosecution for obscenity. Countless popular

Rustam kneeling in grief by his dying son Sohrab. Illustration from a manuscript of *Shahnameh* of 1649.

editions followed, some aimed at children, all feeding the insatiable taste in England for so-called 'Oriental' tales full of the exotic, the flamboyant and the escapist. Coleridge records having been influenced by his early reading of such tales; Wordsworth mentions them in *The Prelude* and Dickens recalls seeking comfort in the same way during his miserable childhood.[7]

The intricacy of *The Thousand and One Nights* has influenced many modern writers the world over, including Salman Rushdie, Italo Calvino, Jorge Luis Borges, A. S. Byatt and Angela Carter, and academic studies have tried to analyse its endless and complex appeal.[8] Sadly the tales are probably best known today as the mangled subjects of pantomimes or parallel fantasy films such as *Sinbad the Sailor*, *Aladdin* and *Ali Baba and the Forty Thieves*, again typifying our failure to engage fully with the wealth of Persian culture.

No discussion of Persian literature would be complete without mention of the bookbinders and illustrators who produced the early manuscripts of works such as the *Shahnameh*. Earlier Persian artwork may have existed but was lost during successive invasions. Certainly in the Islamic period Persian illustrators and decorators of manuscripts became widely celebrated. They became known as miniaturists, referring originally not to the size of their paintings but to the fact that they used red-lead pigment (Latin *minium*). In speaking of those artists, the word 'Persian' must be taken in its widest sense of 'Persian territory', since many of them worked in the courts of provincial rulers in distant parts of the Arab Empire. Baghdad was particularly famous for its artists, although some of them may well have been Persian by birth. Many of them were employed to create work for the Mughal rulers in India and from that connection came Chinese influences to enrich the already complex blend of Indian, Arabic and native Persian styles.[9]

With the drive towards modernization, especially since the early twentieth century, European ideas and European forms of literature such as the novel became more widely known in Persia (Iran). Although some writers embraced this development, others warned against modernization, seeing it as 'Westernization' and posing a threat to traditional culture and historical identity. Jalal Al-e Ahmad, in an influential book published in 1962, stressed this fear, calling Westernization, or 'Westoxication' as it is often translated, 'a disease imported from abroad, and developed in an environment receptive to it'.[10]

Many writers typify the Persian tradition of learning from and adapting other cultural influences. Sadeq Hedayat in novels such as *Buf-e-Kur* (The Blind Owl) is more critical of Islamic influence on Persian life, something that led to the author's persecution and eventual suicide in Paris in 1951. His works were banned completely by the Ahmadinejad regime in 2006, and the same kind of persecution faced other writers too. The result was that any criticism of the clerical rulers has had to be very carefully managed or disguised, and many writers have become exiles in Europe or America.

In the same way, film-makers have had to negotiate the minefield of bans and censorship, which tends to vary from regime to regime. Amazingly, the ban on the staple Western themes of sex and violence has resulted in several films that have won major international awards for their particular quality of poetic simplicity and humanity, often focusing on the roles of women and children in the country's male-dominated society. Again, leading figures such as Abbas Kiarostami have been forced to work abroad, producing work such as *Taste of Cherry* (1997), a film about a man searching for someone to help him to commit suicide, which questions life and Islamic law. In the same way Samira Makhmalbaf in *The Apple* (1998), scripted by her father, Mohsen Makhmalbaf, daringly exposes social injustice and sexual discrimination through the true story of twin sisters who, imprisoned since birth by their ultra-conservative father, finally experience the world at the age of twelve. Again, as so often previously, what stands out is how Iranian film-makers, in spite of difficulties, have entered a new field of culture without losing individuality or national character.

Overall, the outstanding quality of Persian/Iranian culture is its sheer tenacity and vitality. In spite of the numerous seemingly overwhelming moves against it by other powers, ideologies and cultures, it has survived as a complex and individual culture, valuing and preserving the riches of the past but with the courage and confidence to negotiate the restrictions of the present day in a thoughtful and creative manner.

The magnificent palaces of the capital Persepolis were built by Darius I (the Great, *r.* 521–486 BC) around 518 BC. An aerial view of the ruins of Persepolis today.

SIXTEEN

THE FIRST SUPERPOWER?

According to Neil MacGregor, Persia was 'the world superpower of 2,500 years ago', and Cyrus, the first Shahanshah, 'built the largest empire the world had then seen, and changed the world . . . for ever'.[1] However, this Persian Empire was built on different lines from earlier empires in the Middle Eastern region. These had largely imposed their power by the use of brute force. The Persians, however, justified their empire by claiming it was bringing peace and order to the world. They were quite prepared to allow their subject peoples to retain their own religions, languages and general cultural institutions so long as they remained loyal subjects of the Persian Empire and did not disturb its peace. The Persians, constituting the aristocracy of the empire, had their own religion and culture and this distinguished them from the peoples over whom they ruled. They were quite prepared for this distinction to remain. They considered the attributes of their own culture to have been the main contributing factors in their success. Religion was a particular example of such success. As has been observed, the Zoroastrian god Ahuramazda always played a central role in the actions of the Persian superpower.

Arnold Toynbee expressed the opinion that their great imperial success showed that they must have been 'transparently endowed with the classic virtues of "a ruling race"'.[2] Michael Axworthy used the term 'empire of the mind' to describe this.[3] MacGregor considered 'state of mind' to be a more accurate description, since the Achaemenids were bent on the creation of the most effective and enduring imperial state. What they actually devised was a devolved state that, in many ways, was run on federal lines. Thus while this can be credited with creating the first 'universal empire' in recorded history, they simultaneously created the first 'commonwealth of nations'.[4]

The Achaemenids established what was essentially a continental power and their principal means of communication was therefore by land. They were successful in defeating most of the powers of the ancient world, creating their 'universal empire', which covered the greater part of the Middle East and incorporated its ancient civilizations. However, they were never so successful in bringing the adjacent sea peoples of the Mediterranean into their empire, despite many attempts to do so. While their army was immensely powerful, their navy remained weak and they became increasingly dependent on the services of those maritime peoples, such as the Ionian Greeks and the Phoenicians, who had themselves been defeated and incorporated into their empire. They were unable to defeat the Greeks of the peninsula and islands who, at the time of the Achaemenids, controlled most of the eastern Mediterranean.

The conflict between the Persians and the Greeks was the biggest struggle in the ancient world and, viewed from a wider historical perspective, it had considerable significance on the world stage for centuries after. The political geographer Halford Mackinder saw it as being the beginning of a geopolitical pattern that was to be the underlying theme throughout subsequent world history. This was the conflict of land power versus sea power. In an article written in 1904, Mackinder was mainly concerned with the opposition of the two great world empires of the early twentieth century, that is, British and Russian.[5] Since the British Empire was essentially a sea power and Russia was itself a land power, Mackinder saw the conflict between the two as being the latest episode in that great land power–sea power struggle that had begun with the Persians and Greeks more than two thousand years earlier.

Mackinder used the terms 'Landsmen' and 'Seamen' and emphasized that the geographical imperatives of each were and always had been quite different. 'Landsmen' find themselves in a highly challenging physical environment when confronted by the sea, and likewise 'Seamen' are challenged in much the same way when they are confronted by the land.[6] Another theme he considered to be present throughout world history was that the Landsmen were most likely to be the attackers. According to Mackinder, those inhabiting the fastnesses of the 'world island', by which he means Central Asia, attack those who inhabit its maritime fringes. The latter are likely to have become richer and so they become attractive to the Landsmen who, with the limited potential of their environment, are likely to be much less so. The attack by the Persians on the Greeks and the attempt to bring them into their empire was one of the earliest examples of this taking place and was also the first of the many failures by land power to subjugate sea power.[7]

However, the opposite of this took place when Alexander the Great of Macedon defeated the Persians and imposed Hellenic political, economic and cultural norms on the fallen empire, as discussed in Chapter Eight. Hellenic sea power was able to defeat and impose itself for a time on the Persian land power, and it was a Greek world order that emerged from the fall of the Achaemenid Empire. Yet it was not really sea power as such that had accomplished this, but land power acting in conjunction with sea power. The Macedonians were a land people who had been highly influenced by Greek civilization and saw themselves as the protectors and organizers of the otherwise vulnerable Greek world.

This Hellenistic world order did not endure, and in the second century AD a second Persian Empire, that of the Sasanids, emerged. By this time dominance of the Mediterranean had passed from the Greeks to the Romans and a new conflict between the Persians and Romans became the main theme of the next few hundred years of the history of the Mediterranean and Middle East. This rivalry between the principal Mediterranean and major Middle Eastern powers continued until the Islamic conquest.

Despite the huge religious and wider cultural changes brought about by Islam, the maritime–continental rivalry continued at first as Arab–European and then as Turkish–Iberian. It was this that transformed what had been a largely Mediterranean–Middle Eastern conflict into one that took on global dimensions.

While the land–sea conflict can thus be seen as having been an enduring theme throughout world history, there is also an area

between the two that has in many ways been quite as important and at times more so. Mackinder identified this as being the
'Inner Marginal Crescent', but it has more recently been called
the 'Rimland'. This area covers large territories, including much
of Continental Europe and the Middle East. Since Iran is part of
this, it puts it geopolitically in a different position from its earlier
role as the major land power. The countries of this Rimland, such
as France and Germany, have been basically land-oriented but
throughout history have often looked towards the sea as a source
of additional power.

The present Middle East is an area of immense geopolitical
complexity. What was united in the Persian Empire in the fifth
century BC is today split up into over a dozen different, and often
hostile, states. Together with these are a number of independent
city-states, each claiming its own right to the possession of a distinct identity. This geopolitical complexity was actually brought
about by imperial rivalries in the early twentieth century, producing states that in most cases had no real identity at all. The
claims to the possession of identity, particularly those in the Arab
world, are the least plausible. Existing boundaries were drawn by
the imperialists with little reference to physical or human factors,
and much of the violence in the region during the twenty-first
century arises from this fact.

Iran is one of those Middle Eastern states with an indisputably
clear identity based in various complex ways upon its past and
in particular its ancient civilization. Wider cultural features have
been the basis for a strong feeling of nationalism. The last shah, of
course, attempted to transform this into the rebirth of the ancient
Persian Empire. Today in the Islamic Republic of Iran this historic
identity has become closely entwined with Shia Islam, which, as
has been seen, has links with the country's earlier dynasties.

For two centuries the Achaemenids united the ancient world
and became a model for future attempts to bring about peace
through unity. However, with their high level of tolerance they
did not really become a model for future empires. From the time
of the Romans, succeeding empires generally took the approach
of achieving a high level of homogeneity based on chosen cultural

norms. This was far from the system pursued by the ancient Persians, who therefore were the progenitors of a very different type of imperial ambition.

In many ways the Achaemenids may be seen as a kind of model for the twenty-first-century post-imperial world. The 'world' of the ancients was in reality a relatively small part of it, and contemporary globalization has presented the necessity for devising structures on a far larger scale, allowing the establishment of an effective global system. The huge cultural diversity of the world precludes any form of imperial unification along Roman lines, but it does not preclude forms of cooperation and unification on the Persian model. The empire they created was designed to bring peace and to promote the unimpeded functioning of the economy of the ancient world while at the same time allowing a variety of religions and cultures to flourish. This gave a distinct sense of identity to the many different peoples involved, so they were not merely absorbed into an alien universal state that suppressed unique cultures. In order to tackle the global issues in the post-imperial world of the twenty-first century, the emperor certainly needs new clothes.[8]

The political scientist Immanuel Wallerstein believes that from the fifteenth to the twentieth centuries world empires were the dominant feature of the global geopolitical scene; the 'new clothes' that were needed to replace them at the end of the twentieth century were what he termed 'world-economy'. He asserted that 'unlike the world empires [the world-economy] did not possess an overall political structure. It had spread widely over the earth's surface, absorbed the contemporary world empires and created what was, in effect, a single world unit.'[9]

If Wallerstein's analysis has any truth, then it follows that the Achaemenids could be seen as having been not so much the model for future world empires as for their possible successors in the new world system. To bring about a transformation from the complex and violent world of the early twenty-first century to a more peaceful and productive one, the great state that dominated the ancient world over two millennia earlier could yet prove to have much to offer as a guide for the future of humanity.

POWER AND
PARADISE

Ancient Persian civilization is so bound up with Cyrus the Great that if we attempt to find the geographical heart of the Achaemenid Empire we need look no further than Pasargadae. There the great victory over the Medes began the Persian rise to a dominant position in the Middle East, and there also is the tomb of the victor himself. Over the centuries many of the great and the good, from Alexander the Great to the last shah, and more recently Ayatollah Khamene'i, now supreme leader of the Islamic Republic, have come to pay their respects. Pasargadae was also the place that Cyrus chose as his capital. Whatever regime has subsequently been in power in Persia, Cyrus and his tomb at Pasargadae have always been accorded due respect.

The tomb of Cyrus is now visited by large numbers of people who are likely to visit at the same time as seeing the tomb of his successor, Darius, which is nearby. The *pairidaēza* has long disappeared and Cyrus's tomb now stands in solitary – but splendid – isolation on the bleak plain of Pars. However, it is not completely alone. Adjacent to the small road leading to the tomb stands a secondary school for boys. Outside this school a large sign in English reads: 'Welcome to the land of the freeborn poets, devouts, philosophers and heroes. Pasargad High School'. This sign is clearly intended to make a statement about how modern Iran views its ancient heritage. It links the youth of the Islamic Republic with the achievements of Persian/Iranian civilization over the millennia. The poets, devouts, philosophers and heroes are clearly seen as part of a long and illustrious national history. It is recognized that these

Iranian visitors to the Tomb of Cyrus.

Pasargad High School.

poets and others of earlier generations all made their particular contributions to the identity of Iran.

While today Iran is an Islamic Republic, many other ideas and ideologies have prevailed at different periods in the country's history. However, underlying them all has been a feeling of identity that emphasizes the country itself and its individuality. It is possible to perceive this in ancient times in Zoroastrianism, the religion of the Achaemenid dynasty. One can also see it much later in Shia Islam, in many ways an assertion of the role of Persians and their ideas in the development of the religion. The importance of this native contribution to Islam has been further explored by scholars since the Khomeini revolution. Most recently Patricia Crone's research on the 'nativist prophets' has stressed their importance in converting 'Islamic Persia' into 'Persian Islam'. Her thesis that indigenous rural prophets in Iran had defied conquering Arabs and helped to shape a distinct Islamic culture is one with an obvious appeal to Persian nationalism.

The Tomb of Cyrus and Pasargad High School, geographically so close together on the plain of Pars, are separated in time by well over two millennia. They are nevertheless linked by the strong feeling of national identity that has persisted, despite the massive upheavals that have taken place in the country. From the earliest times, the 'devouts and philosophers', together with the poets, have provided a sense of unity throughout the long history of the country. Implicit in this is the acceptance of the existence of diversity. Such acceptance may not be all that apparent at any particular period, but it can be seen clearly when viewed in the wider context of history.

In attempting to explain this diversity, it has been observed that there are in some ways two countries, Persia and Iran, occupying the same geographical space. Each of these has presented over time a very different image. Michael Axworthy sets out what he calls this 'paradox' as follows: 'The image conjured up by Persia is one of romance; roses and nightingales in elegant gardens . . . carpets with colours glowing like jewels, poetry and melodious music.' On the other hand, in the modern media in particular, 'Iran has a rather different image: frowning mullahs, black oil, women's blanched faces peering . . . from under black chadors, grim crowds burning flags, chanting "death to".'[1]

And yet the two images are by no means irreconcilable, and this unity in diversity is perhaps the most outstanding characteristic of Iran. It explains the way in which the ancient civilization has been lost many times but found again by future generations, usually with very different ideas. During the 1980s, after paying a visit to Persepolis and Pasargadae, the Ayatollah Khamene'i spoke of 'monuments which after the lapse of tens of centuries still remain a marvel to mankind'. They are a treasury, he said, in which we can see history and humanity. The Ayatollah was talking about the wider context of history in which ultimately it is possible to detect distinct themes running through the complexity.

Iran's foundations may have been in the remote past but the relevance of these foundations has persisted in supporting a national framework for the ideas of each new generation. In this way a distinct Iranian identity has been preserved in one of the most highly volatile regions in the world.

1 Origins: The Land and the People

1 In the eighteenth century the earliest translations of Sanskrit texts were beginning to arrive in the West, notably Anquetil Duperron's translation of the Avesta. His work was taken up by Sir William Jones, a judge in the Indian judicial system, who initiated the study of comparative philology, which led to the idea of a seminal language that came to be called Indo-European or Aryan.
2 John Keay, *India: A History* (London, 2000), p. 21.

2 The Achaemenid Dynasty

1 In 597 BC Jerusalem fell to Nebuchadnezzar II of Babylon. He returned with a large number of Jews, who were kept imprisoned as slaves. This 'Babylonian Captivity' continued until 538 BC when Cyrus, having defeated the Babylonian prince Belshazzar, had the prisoners released and permitted them to return to their homeland. This has since been regarded as an act of great benevolence by Cyrus, a figure synonymous with good in the biblical texts.
2 A 'forward' capital as identified by Vaughan Cornish for the purpose of further advance in that direction and or defence against a strong and hostile foe. See Vaughan Cornish, *The Great Capitals: An Historical Geography* (London, 1923) and Chapter Nine, note 2.
3 There are many accounts of how this took place. See Chapter Four.
4 Herodotus, *The Histories*, trans. A. de Sélincourt, revd J. Marincola (London, 1996). Much of what we know about the Persians actually comes from their great enemy, the Greeks. This does not mean that Persia would inevitably be seen in a bad light. On the contrary, the Greeks felt considerable admiration for the Persians, and much of what was said by Herodotus and others was often more favourable to the Persians than it was to the Greeks.
5 The Greek word *oikoumene* used in this sense originally meant the habitat of mankind. Arnold Toynbee talked of the 'old world

oikoumene' as being the Mediterranean–Middle Eastern region, which he saw as having possessed a fundamental historical unity. See Arnold Toynbee, *Mankind and Mother Earth: A Narrative History of the World* (London, 1976), chapter Four. In modern times, the term *oecoumene* or *ecumene* has been used rather generally to indicate the centre of the inhabited world. The universal state in the sense used here would be the state that established a position of dominance over the *ecumene*. See Geoffrey Parker, *The Geopolitics of Domination* (London, 1988), pp. 9–10.

6 Herodotus, *Histories*, p. 417.
7 G. Regan, *Battles that Changed History* (London, 2002), p. 11.

3 THE ACHIEVEMENTS OF THE ACHAEMENIDS

1 Arnold Toynbee, *Mankind and Mother Earth* (London, 1976), p. 184.
2 Herodotus, *The Histories*, trans. A. de Sélincourt, revd J. Marincola (London, 1996), p. 533.
3 R. N. Sharp, *The Inscriptions in Old Persian Cuneiform of the Achaemenian Emperors*, Central Council for the Celebrations of the 25th Century of the Foundation of the Iranian Empire (Tehran, 1971), p. 96.
4 Neil MacGregor, *A History of the World in 100 Objects* (London, 2010), pp. 165–70.
5 Herodotus, *Histories*, p. 588.

4 CYRUS THE GREAT IN HISTORY AND LEGEND

1 Herodotus, *The Histories*, trans. A. de Sélincourt, revd J. Marincola (London, 1996), p. 3.
2 Another version was that a sudden storm put out the flames and this was taken as a sign that Croesus should be spared.
3 The river that Herodotus called the Araxes would have been generally known in antiquity as the Oxus. Persian influence was being extended northwards into those lands from which the Aryans had originally expanded outwards. Known today as the Amu Darya, it flows from the Tien Shan mountains into the Aral Sea and forms part of Transoxiana, a large Central Asian river basin.
4 A. Baehrens, *Poetae Latini Minores* (Leipzig, 1883), vol. v, p. 402.
5 Unlike Herodotus, in *The Persians* Aeschylus was dealing with a contemporary event. He is said to have fought at the battle of Marathon and probably also Salamis. This means that he was an active participant in the events depicted and he would have reflected the common attitudes to them at the time of writing.
6 Aeschylus, 'The Persians', trans. S. G. Benardete, in *The Complete Greek Tragedies*, ed. David Grene et al., vol. I (Chicago, IL, 1956).
7 Quoted in J. Curtis, *Ancient Persia* (London, 2013), p. 41.
8 Arthur M. Young, *Echoes of Two Cultures* (Pittsburgh, PA, 1964), p. 12.

9 G. L. Hunter, *The Practical Book of Tapestries* (Philadelphia, PA, 1925), p. 226.
10 Young, *Echoes of Two Cultures*, p. 54.

5 Persepolis: City, Throne and Power

1 See Chapter Fifteen for further information on the *Shahnameh*.
2 J. Gloag, *The Architectural Interpretation of History* (London, 1975), p. 58.
3 R. N. Sharp, *The Inscriptions in Old Persian Cuneiform of the Achaemenian Emperors*, Central Council for the Celebrations of the 25th Century of the Foundation of the Iranian Empire (Tehran, 1971), p. 87.
4 W. H. Forbis, *The Fall of the Peacock Throne* (New York and London, 1980), p. 57.
5 Sharp, *Inscriptions in Old Persian Cuneiform*, p. 87.
6 J. Hicks, *The Emergence of Man: The Persians* (New York, 1975), p. 28.
7 G. Parker, *Power in Stone: Cities as Symbols of Empire* (London, 2014), Chapter Fourteen.

6 Thus Spake Zarathustra: Religion and Empire

1 The uncertainty concerning Zarathustra's place of birth is demonstrated by the fact that he has also been claimed by many other places as far afield as Azerbaijan in the west and Transoxiana in the north.
2 Zurvanism developed in order to tackle the problems of good and evil inherent in Zoroastrianism. This version of the religion was most influential during the period of the Sasanian dynasty.
3 Mithra and Mithraism came to be better known in Europe well after the end of the Achaemenid dynasty through its incorporation into the pantheon of Roman gods. Mithras became much favoured by the Roman army and was very much associated with the military throughout the Roman Empire. A temple of Mithras was excavated by archaeologists in London in the 1950s and from this much was learned of the Mithraic tradition.
4 R. Ghirshman, *Iran* (London, 1954), p. 162.
5 The gold tablet of Ariaramnes is now in the Pergamon Museum in Berlin.
6 Inscription at Persepolis, translated by R. N. Sharp in *The Inscriptions in Old Persian Cuneiform of the Achaemenian Emperors*, Central Council for the Celebrations of the 25th Century of the Foundation of the Iranian Empire (Tehran, 1971).
7 Paul Kriwaczek, *In Search of Zarathustra* (London, 2002), pp. 26–30.

7 Paradise Gained

1 Aryan became a general name used for the peoples of Central Asia. The word is actually Sanskrit and means noble or high born. In the Indian context, this indicated that these people came as conquerors, quickly

dominating the native peoples of South Asia. The linguistic evidence demonstrates that they were closely related to both the Romans and many of the migratory peoples of southwest Asia. During the twentieth century it became associated particularly with the prevalent racism of the time.

2 D. R. Lightfoot, 'The Origin and Diffusion of Qanats in Arabia: New Evidence from the Northern and Southern Peninsula', *Geographical Journal*, CLXVI/3 (2000).

3 Ronald King, *The Quest for Paradise: A History of the World's Gardens* (Weybridge, 1979), p. 21.

4 The Old Persian *pairidaēza* derives from the two words *pairi* (around) and *daēza* (wall).

5 *Encyclopedia of World Religions* (London, 1975), p. 174.

6 Xenophon, *Oeconomicus*, Book IV, trans. E. C. Marchant (Cambridge, MA, 1923).

7 King, *Quest for Paradise*, p. 25.

8 Ibid., p. 22.

9 Paul Kriwaczek, *In Search of Zarathustra* (London, 2002), p. 8.

10 Lightfoot, 'Origin and Diffusion of Qanats in Arabia'.

8 Alexander of Macedon and the Hellenistic Interlude

1 G. Regan, *Battles that Changed History: Fifty Decisive Battles Spanning Over 2,500 Years of Warfare* (London, 2002), pp. 18–19.

2 Ibid., p. 20.

3 Arnold Toynbee, *A Study of History*, vol. V (Oxford, 1939), pp. 47–58.

4 The Sogdians were a people whose territory was in upper Transoxiana and who had been conquered originally by Cyrus himself. Throughout the Achaemenid period they had been either in the empire or highly influenced by Persia and its culture. In this way their relationship to the Persians was similar to that of the Macedonians to the Greeks.

5 The early death of the great conqueror has been put down to many different causes. It certainly seems that on his arrival in Babylon he engaged in a huge bout of drinking, which must have weakened him. After this he developed a fever from which he failed to recover. Another suggestion was that he was poisoned. Whatever the cause, his death put an end to the great aim of unifying the ancient world under Hellenic control and so creating a fitting successor state to the Achaemenid Empire. See T. Gergel, ed., *Alexander the Great: Selected Texts from Arrian, Curtius and Plutarch* (London and New York, 2004), pp. 137–45.

6 Ibid., p. 143.

7 Geoffrey Parker, *Sovereign City: The City State Through History* (London, 2004), pp. 53–4.

8 Ibid., p. 56.

9 Ibid., p. 50.

9 Empire Revived: The Sasanids

1 Geoffrey Parker, *Power in Stone: Cities as Symbols of Empire* (London, 2014), Chapter Three.

2 Vaughan Cornish, *The Great Capitals: An Historical Geography* (London, 1923), pp. 36–59. Cornish proposed the theory of the 'forward capital', which was a capital situated close to the most dynamic or endangered frontier. Such a capital would be well located to direct military activity in the frontier areas. If the frontier was an expanding one and as a result territory was gained, the capital would sometimes be moved even closer to the frontier to keep as close as possible to the new theatre of operations. This might even take it for a time into territory still claimed by the opposing power.

3 'The Laws of the Medes and the Persians' had been one of the main unifying features of the otherwise devolved Achaemenid Empire. As has been seen, the Medes had very much been the mentors of the Persians in the creation of their empire, and a common legal system was something that was always considered an essential feature of empire.

4 The German Schlieffen Plan was the brainchild of General von Schlieffen, who was commander of the German army before the First World War. Faced with the possibility of war on two fronts, east and west, the plan was to attack what was perceived to be the weaker power, France, and, having defeated that power, to move the might of the German army eastwards to deal with the far more formidable Russian threat. While Schlieffen had his priorities wrong, Shapur got them right.

5 'Sacred space' is a term used in political geography to describe an area with very special associations for a people. It is likely to have been their first homeland and, although it may have lost its former importance in real terms, it has a special historical and cultural significance.

6 R. N. Sharp, *The Inscriptions in Old Persian Cuneiform of the Achaemenian Emperors*, Central Council for the Celebrations of the 25th Century of the Foundation of the Iranian Empire (Tehran, 1971), p. 96.

7 Manichaeism was the religion of the prophet Mani, who was born into a Christian family near Ctesiphon just before the Sasanian victory over the Parthians. The religion he preached was a kind of fusion of Christianity, Buddhism and Zoroastrianism. However, its dominant doctrine, the confrontation of good and evil, light and darkness, certainly owed most to the Zoroastrian tradition.

10 Islamic Persia and Persian Islam

1 This was all very similar to the Norman invaders of England in the eleventh century. They inherited the wealth and estates of their Anglo-Saxon predecessors and in this way established themselves as a new ruling class. Since they had secured the blessing of the pope for their enterprise, that conquest also had a religious dimension. Nevertheless,

the Anglo-Saxon culture survived and evolved into what eventually became English culture.

2 Alessandro Bausani, *The Persians*, trans. J. B Donne (London, 1971), pp. 71–2.

3 Geoffrey Parker, *Power in Stone: Cities as Symbols of Empire* (London, 2014), pp. 48–9.

4 The *Shuubiyya* movement is sometimes seen as having been a debate among theologians and intellectuals and sometimes as a wider proto-nationalist movement. According to H.A.R. Gibb, it was very much a debate over the position of Persia within Islam. He considered that it was a question of whether Islamic society 'was to become a re-embodiment of the old Perso-Aramaic culture into which Arabic and Islamic elements would be absorbed, or a culture in which the Perso-Aramean contributions would be subordinated to the Arab tradition and Islamic values'. Of course the *Shuubiyya* wished the historic Persian culture to prevail and bent all its efforts to this end. H.A.R. Gibb, 'The Social Significance of the *Shuubiyya*', in *Studia Oriental Ioanni Pedersen* (Copenhagen, 1954), p. 108.

5 The word 'Assassin' was used by the Crusaders and derives from the Arabic *Hashshashin*, the takers of hashish. This drug seems to have been used by them not only in rituals but to give to those chosen to commit the murders so that they would be in the right frame of mind.

11 FROM PERSEPOLIS TO SAMARKAND: THE PERSIAN LEGACY IN CENTRAL ASIA

1 At the very beginning of the Achaemenid Empire, Cyrus had been concerned with security on the northern borders. In order to protect these he had invaded Central Asia. There he had come up against the Massagetae and it was in battle with them that he was killed. This episode demonstrated very clearly the danger that always came from this direction.

2 The Silk Road was not a road at all. It is a collective name for a number of routes that linked together the western and the eastern parts of Eurasia. Many Central Asian rulers desired that the route should pass through their territories and one of the most successful of these routeways remained that through Transoxiana.

3 The Turks were, in fact, early converts to Islam. They had made contact with the Arabs in the early eighth century and soon converted to Islam. It was they who took Islam eastwards towards China and established the religion firmly throughout Central Asia. By the time of the Samanids the region had been thoroughly permeated by Islam.

4 H. M. Said and A. S. Khan, *Al Biruni, His Times, Life and Works*, Hamdard Foundation (Karachi, 1981), p. 47.

5 The Koran was in Arabic and so throughout the Islamic world this language had to be learned. All religious study in the madrasas was invariably in Arabic. As a result, after the Arabic conquest, Persian

was relegated to being the language used in the home and in the day-to-day activities of the people.

6 Timur came to be best known to Elizabethan England through the play *Tamburlaine the Great* by Christopher Marlowe.

7 Much information about Timur and his activities comes to us from foreign travellers, including ambassadors. Ruy Gonzáles de Clavijo was one of the most informative of these.

8 J. Ure, *The Trail of Tamerlane* (London, 1980), p. 170.

9 W. H. Forbis, *Fall of the Peacock Throne* (New York and London, 1980), p. 65.

10 Ure, *The Trail of Tamerlane*, p. 191.

11 J. Marozzi, *Tamerlane: Sword of Islam, Conqueror of the World* (London, 2004), p. 33.

12 Quoted ibid., p. 201.

13 Luc Kwanten, *Imperial Nomads: A History of Central Asia, 500–1500* (Philadelphia, PA, 1979), p. 268.

14 Marozzi, *Tamerlane*, pp. 210, 277.

15 R. Grousset, *A History of Asia*, trans. D. Scott (New York, 1963), p. 88.

12 PARADISE OF BLISS: THE PERSIAN LEGACY IN INDIA FROM THE TIMURIDS TO THE MUGHALS

1 C. Irving, *Crossroads of Civilisation: 3,000 Years of Persian History* (London, 1979), p. 71.

2 George Curzon, quoted in J. Marozzi, *Tamerlane: Sword of Islam, Conqueror of the World* (London, 2004), p. 222.

3 R. Grousset, *A History of Asia*, trans. D. Scott (New York, 1963), pp. 89–90.

4 Quoted in K. Hopkirk, *Central Asia: A Traveller's Companion* (London, 1993), p. 163.

5 V. A. Smith, *The Oxford History of India*, ed. P. Spear (Oxford, 1982), p. 320.

6 Despite the great Persian heritage of the Timurids, Babur always regarded himself as a Turk. The *Babur-nama* was originally written in Turkish but was transcribed by his son Humayun and translated into Persian under the direction of his grandson Akbar. It was first translated from Persian into English by John Leyden and William Erskine in 1836.

7 Geoffrey Parker, *Power in Stone: Cities as Symbols of Empire* (London, 2014), pp. 108–9.

8 Ibid, p. 110.

9 J. Keay, *India: A History* (London, 2000), pp. 311–15.

10 The many cities built over the millennia on the site of Delhi gave rise to the tradition of the 'seven cities' of Delhi. In fact there were more than seven and each of them came to symbolize a particular regime or empire. Parker, *Power in Stone*, Chapter Six.

11 L. Nicholson, *The Red Fort, Delhi* (London, 1989), p. 80.

12 François Bernier, *Travels in the Mogul Empire, AD 1656–1668* [1670], trans. A. Constable (Oxford, 1916), pp. 60–70.

13 Keay, *India*, pp. 310–11.

14 The idea of the 'East' as being homogeneous and different was something very basic in Victorian geopolitical thinking. Rudyard Kipling expressed this in his poem 'The Ballad of East and West': 'Oh, East is East and West is West, and never the twain shall meet. / Till Earth and Sky stand presently at God's great Judgment Seat.' The whole concept has been re-evaluated by post-colonial theorists, such as Edward Said in his book *Orientalism* (London, 1978).

15 Following the deposition of the last shah, the Peacock Throne was removed from the Royal Palace. It is currently in the vaults of the National Bank in Tehran and is not on public display.

13 CYRUS WITH GOLDEN CAVIAR: THE LAST DYNASTY SALUTES THE FIRST

1 Lord Curzon saw Persia as being 'one of the pieces on a chessboard upon which is being played out a game for the dominion of the world. The future of Great Britain . . . will be decided, not in Europe, not even upon the seas and oceans which are swept by her flag, or in the Greater Britain which has been called into existence by her offspring, but in the continent where our emigrant stock first came, and to which as conquerors their descendants have returned. Without India the British Empire could not exist.' G. N. Curzon, *Persia and the Persian Question* (London, 1966), p. 10.

2 The existence of oil in Persia had been known over the millennia, as it was the substance that fuelled the Zoroastrian fire temples. The ease with which fires could be lit and maintained must have been a factor in the importance of fire in that religion.

3 The choice of Pahlavi as the dynastic name was a deliberate attempt to invoke the glorious past of pre-Islamic Persia. During the Parthian period their tongue came to be called *pahlavanik* (heroic) and this persisted through the Sasanid period. This distinguished Middle Persian from the Old Persian of the Achaemenids. The word survives in modern Persian as *pahlavan*, meaning hero or brave man.

4 W. M. Shuster, *The Strangling of Persia* (London, 1912). Morgan Shuster, an advisor to the American government on Persian affairs, hated the British Empire and his harsh judgement on British policy in Persia was a product of the rise of the USA as a world power. His book had a considerable influence on the policies of the new dynasty.

5 In the early twentieth century, racialist ideas were widespread. In Europe, and most especially in Germany, one of the most vicious aspects of this was anti-Semitism, which eventually led to the Holocaust during the Second World War. Reza Shah was highly embarrassed by the weakness of his country, and in these circumstances it is not really at all surprising that, desirous of bringing back its former greatness, he should have attracted the racialism that included the Iranians as an Aryan people.

6 John A. Boyle, *Persia: History and Heritage* (London, 1978), p. 64.

7 J. Lowe et al., *Celebration at Persepolis* (Geneva, 1971), quoted in Patrick Clawson and Michael Rubin, *Eternal Iran: Continuity and Chaos* (New York, 2005), p. 78.

8 Paul Kriwaczek, *In Search of Zarathustra* (London, 2002), p. 171.

9 Michael Axworthy, *Iran: Empire of the Mind* (London, 2008), p. 256.

10 Quoted in Kriwaczek, *In Search of Zarathustra*, p. 11.

11 The cost was certainly immense and is said to have been as much as $200 million. Rather than being the celebration of the return of greatness under the Pahlavis, the emptying of the exchequer marked the beginning of the end of the dynasty. James A. Bill, *The Eagle and the Lion: The Tragedy of American–Iranian Relations* (London, 1988), pp. 133–4.

14 From Shahyad to Azadi: The Islamic Republic and the Ancient Legacy

1 Patrick Clawson and Michael Rubin, *Eternal Iran: Continuity and Chaos* (New York, 2005), pp. 99–100.

2 Koorosh-e Kamali-e Sarvestani, *Fars*, Foundation for Fars Province Studies, trans. R. Parhizgar (Shiraz, 1996), p. 7.

3 M. Rastegare Fasai, *Farsnameh*, Ebn-e Balkhi (Shiraz, 1995), pp. 50–51.

4 Sarvestani, *Fars*, p. 10.

5 S. A. Khamene'i, *Takhte-Jamshid (Persepolis)*, Iranian Cultural Heritage Organisation (1988), pp. 1–2.

6 Quoted in Lindsey A. Allen, *The Persian Empire* (London, 2005), p. 184.

7 L. P. Elwell-Sutton, 'The Pahlavi Era', in *Persia: History and Heritage*, ed. John A. Boyle (London, 1978), p. 64.

15 Lost in Translation?

1 Word similarities that support this view of a common root language include *pedar* (father), see Latin *pater*; *dokhta* (daughter), see German *Tochter*; *tondar* (thunder); *madar* (mother) and *mordan*; see French *mort* (death).

2 Paul Kriwaczek, *In Search of Zarathustra* (London, 2002), pp. 36–45.

3 John Curtis, *Ancient Persia* (London, 2013), pp. 84–7.

4 Roger Stevens, *The Land of the Great Sophy*, 2nd edn (London, 1971), pp. 32–3.

5 Michael Wood, *In the Footsteps of Alexander the Great* (London, 1997), p. 119.

6 Farnoosh Moshiri, *The Drum Tower* (Dingwall, 2014).

7 William Wordsworth, *The Prelude*, Book v (Oxford, 1970); Charles Dickens, 'A Christmas Tree', *Household Words*, Extra Christmas Number (1850).

8 Serious attempts to appreciate the full complexity of *The Arabian Nights* and its influence on subsequent literature include Peter L. Caracciolo, ed., *The Arabian Nights in English Literature* (Basingstoke, 1988), and Robert Irwin, *The Arabian Nights: A Companion* (London, 1994).

9 An interesting glimpse into the world of the miniaturists may be seen in a novel by the modern Turkish writer Orhan Pamuk, *My Name is Red*, trans. Erdağ M. Göknar (London, 2001).

10 Jalal al-e Ahmad, *Occidentosis: A Plague from the West*, trans. R. Campbell (Berkeley, CA, 1984).

16 THE FIRST SUPERPOWER?

1 Neil MacGregor, *A History of the World in 100 Objects* (London, 2010), pp. 165–6.

2 Arnold Toynbee, *A Study of History*, vol. V (Oxford, 1939), pp. 47–8.

3 Michael Axworthy, *Iran: Empire of the Mind* (London, 2008).

4 Brian Dicks, *The Ancient Persians: How They Lived and Worked* (London, 1979), p. 9.

5 H. Mackinder, 'The Geographical Pivot of History', *Geographical Journal*, XXIII (1904).

6 H. Mackinder, 'The Seaman's Point of View' and 'The Landsman's Point of View', in *Democratic Ideals and Reality* (London and New York, 1919).

7 The more vulnerable sea peoples in the ancient world were in fact conquered by the Persians. The Ionian Greeks of Anatolia and the Phoenicians of the eastern Mediterranean coast were subjugated and incorporated by the Achaemenids. The Ionian Greeks were then supported by the Athenians and their neighbours and became a major factor in the Persian determination to defeat them and bring them into their empire.

8 Hans Christian Andersen, 'The Emperor's New Clothes' (1837). In this story, the emperor appears in what he thinks are the finest robes he has ever worn. The reality, as is pointed out by one small child in the watching crowd, is that he is not wearing any clothes at all. This can be taken as a metaphor for the twenty-first-century world in which fresh thinking and completely new geopolitical clothing is needed. See Geoffrey Parker, 'The Emperor's New Clothes: Radical Alternatives in Contemporary Thought', in Parker, *Western Geopolitical Thought in the Twentieth Century* (London, 1985).

9 Parker, *Western Geopolitical Thought*, p. 157.

CONCLUSION: POWER AND PARADISE

1 M. Axworthy, *Iran: Empire of the Mind* (London, 2008), p. xv.

■▨▧ BIBLIOGRAPHY

Abrahamian, Ervand, *Iran Between Two Revolutions* (Princeton, NJ, 1982)
Allen, Lindsey, *The Persian Empire: A History* (London, 2005)
Arberry, A. J., *Classical Persian Literature* (London, 2004)
—, trans. and ed., *The Rubaiyat of Omar Khayyam* (London, 1949)
—, trans., *Scheherazade: Tales from the Thousand and One Nights*
    (London, 1953)
Arjomand, S. A., *The Turban for the Crown* (Oxford, 1988)
Axworthy, Michael, *Iran: Empire of the Mind* (London, 2008)
Bausani, Alessandro, *Religion in Iran* (New York, 2000)
—, *The Persians*, trans. J. B. Donne (London, 1971)
Boyce, Mary, *A History of Zoroastrianism* (Leiden, 1975)
Boyle, John A., ed., *Persia: History and Heritage* (London, 1978)
Clawson, Patrick, and Michael Rubin, *Eternal Iran: Continuity and Chaos*
    (New York, 2005)
Cornish, Vaughan, *The Great Capitals: An Historical Geography* (London, 1923)
Crone, P., *The Nativist Prophets of Early Islamic Iran* (London, 2012)
Curtis, J., *Ancient Persia* (London, 2013)
—, and N. Tallis, eds, *Forgotten Empire: The World of Ancient Persia*
    (London, 2005)
—, and St J. Simpson, *The World of Achaemenid Persia* (London, 2010)
Curtis, Vesta Sarkhosh, *Persian Myths* (London, 2009)
—, and S. Stewart, eds, *The Birth of the Persian Empire: The Idea of Iran*, vol. I
    (London, 2005)
Curzon, G. N., *Persia and the Persian Question* (London, 1966)
Dicks, Brian, *The Ancient Persians: How they Lived and Worked* (London, 1979)
Ferrier, R. W., *The Art of Persia* (New Haven, CT, 1989)
Forbis, W. H., *The Fall of the Peacock Throne* (New York and London, 1980)
Frye, Richard N., *The Golden Age of Persia* (London, 1993)
—, *The Heritage of Persia* (London, 1976)
Ghirshman, R., *Iran: From the Earliest Times to the Islamic Conquest*
    (London, 1978)
Gnoli, Gherardo, *The Idea of Iran: An Essay on its Origins* (Rome, 1989)

Herodotus, *The Histories*, trans. A. de Sélincourt, revd J. Marincola
    (London, 1996)

Herrmann, Georgina, *The Iranian Revival* (Oxford, 1977)

Hicks, J., *The Emergence of Man: The Persians* (New York, 1975)

Holland, Tom, *Persian Fire: The First World Empire and the Battle for the West*
    (London, 2006)

Irving, C., *Crossroads of Civilisation: 3000 Years of Persian History*
    (London, 1979)

King, Peter, ed., *Curzon's Persia* (London, 1986)

King, Ronald, *The Quest for Paradise: A History of the World's Gardens*
    (Weybridge, 1979)

Kriwaczek, Paul, *In Search of Zarathustra* (London, 2002)

MacGregor, Neil, *A History of the World in 100 Objects* (London, 2010)

Martin, Vanessa, *Islam and Modernism* (London, 1989)

Matheson, Sylvia A., *Persia: An Archaeological Guide* (London, 1972)

Olmstead, A. T., *History of the Persian Empire* (Chicago, 1960)

Parker, G., *Power in Stone: Cities as Symbols of Empire* (London, 2014)

—, *Sovereign City: The City State Through History* (London, 2004)

Tapper, Richard, ed., *The New Iranian Cinema: Politics, Representation
    and Identity* (London, 2002)

Toynbee, Arnold, *A Study of History*, vol. v (Oxford, 1939)

—, *Mankind and Mother Earth: A Narrative History of the World* (Oxford, 1976)

Washington, Peter, ed., *Persian Poems* (London, 2000)

Waters, Matt, *Ancient Persia: A Concise History of the Achaemenid Empire*
    (Cambridge, 2014)

Wiesehöfer, Josef, *Ancient Persia* (London, 2006)

Wright, Denis, *The English Among the Persians* (London, 1977)

Young, Arthur M., *Echoes of Two Cultures* (Pittsburgh, 1964)

ACKNOWLEDGEMENTS

The authors would like to acknowledge the assistance of colleagues in the universities of Tehran and Shiraz in making available sources of material which proved to be very relevant to this book. Also to Ben Hayes, the commissioning editor, for his active participation in the planning of the book and especially for his work on the images. The assistance of our daughter Julie Parker-Mason has been invaluable at many stages in the writing of the book.

Geoffrey Parker wishes to thank the University of Birmingham and the British Council for their help in enabling him to pay a number of visits to Iran.

▚ PHOTO ACKNOWLEDGEMENTS

The author and publishers wish to express their thanks to the below sources of illustrative material and/or permission to reproduce it. Some locations of artworks are also given below.

Photographs by the author: pp. 21, 33, 39, 46, 62, 63, 65, 68, 71, 76, 77, 100, 103, 106, 129, 143, 144, 154, 165, 190, 191; © Sebastian Ballard: pp. 19, 31; © Getty Images: pp. 158, 159; © Museum Associates/LACMA: pp. 42, 66, 151, 173; Library of Congress, Prints and Photographs Division: p. 131; Musée du Louvre, Paris: p. 12; © MET: pp. 38, 40, 55, 176; courtesy of the *Geographical Journal*: p. 83; courtesy of Sotheby's, London: p. 16; NYPL: pp. 139, 179.